Reciprocity
and the position of women

J. VAN BAAL

Reciprocity
and the position of women

ANTHROPOLOGICAL PAPERS

1975

Van Gorcum, Assen/Amsterdam, The Netherlands

ISBN 90 232 1320 3

Printed in the Netherlands by Van Gorcum, Assen

Preface

Reciprocity is the golden rule for human behaviour in all interpersonal relations, but reciprocity is not always as strictly balanced as the word suggests. Often the balance is muddled, sometimes even clearly absent, and all this not by disobedience to social rules, but because the rules themselves prescribe a certain measure of imbalance. The first of the three papers here presented, examines why reciprocity is more strictly balanced in trade and in the adjudication of civil law than it is in the exchange of gifts and the administration of justice in criminal cases.

The second, and more in particular the third paper, are concerned with a specific case of poorly balanced reciprocity, that ensuing from the low social position of women. The assumption that this low position of women is due to the comparative unimportance of their contributions to the economy of the group, is flatly contradicted by the fact that in many simple societies the women contribute at least twice as much as the men do to the economy of the household (the only economy there is in such societies) and still are underprivileged socially. Why are they? Why do they accept it? Although it is appropriate to raise such questions in the year that has been proclaimed the Year of the Woman, this is certainly not the context in which these questions have been brought up. Perhaps the advocates of women's rights will find here some-

5

thing to their taste, but they will hardly be interested in the hypothesis, forwarded in *The Part of Women in the Marriage-trade*, that the notion of matrilineal descent owes more to virilocal than to matrilocal marriage. Nor can they be expected to welcome a hypothetical model of early human society like the one discussed in the third paper where I suggest that, if ever there was question of expelling members of the younger generation from the group, it were not the fathers who chased their sons away, but the mothers who wished to get rid of their daughters.

Although there is a certain measure of consistency in the contents of the three papers, their coherence should not be over-emphasized. They were written at different times and for different purposes. The first was composed as a contribution to an anthropology in modules to be published in the United States. When the original plan collapsed I found the present publishers, Van Gorcum & Comp., willing to publish the paper, together with the two others, a willingness that confirms a lasting and friendly relationship for which I here express my sincere thanks.

The second paper was first published in 1970, in vol. 126 of the *Bijdragen tot de Taal-, Land- en Volkenkunde* (pp. 289-308). I thank the Board of the Koninklijk Instituut voor Taal-, Land- en Volkenkunde at Leiden for their kind permission to reprint the article in the present volume, where it appears in slightly modified form.

The final paper was written recently, in part as an afterthought to the former, in part in reaction to two recent ethnographies that forcibly redirected my attention to the contradictions inherent to the position of women in many parts of the world.

Among those to whom I feel indebted I wish to

mention first of all Professor James L. Peacock of the University of North Carolina who persuaded me to write on reciprocity, a task which I found highly rewarding. I also thank Mrs. Stephanie L. Pinson of New Jersey, U.S.A., for her corrections of my use of the English language and its adaptation to American usage in the paper on Reciprocity.

Many thanks are due to Mr. W. E. A. van Beek and Mr. A. de Ruyter, both of the Institute of Cultural Anthropology of Utrecht State University, for their support, and their comments and suggestions with regard to the drafts of the first two papers. Above all, however, I am indebted to my friend and colleague of Leiden University, Professor P. E. de Josselin de Jong, for the various ways by which he contributed to the realization of the present publication.

J. van Baal

Table of contents

I

Reciprocity

1 *Introduction*

Reciprocity is doing or rendering something in return for a good received, an act committed, or an evil inflicted. Involved is an exchange in which the term has connotations of approximate equivalence and equality. In our culture reciprocity is held to be the basic principle of prescribed or desired behavior in interpersonal relations. The absence or occasional imbalance of reciprocity is often experienced as a wrong, and much thought has been given to social inequality and the unequal distribution of power as possible causes of deviations from the rule of reciprocity. Since anthropology is an empirical discipline, the discussions of the various schools of moral and political philosophy are not our concern here, except as they influence our notions of the life of early man, who was depicted by Thomas Hobbes (1651) as amoral, living in a state of war of all against everyone, and by J.-J. Rousseau as a noble savage who lived in blissful peace until the state of society pressed upon him the many inequalities that modern democracy seeks to overcome. The corresponding ideal types of the amoral savage and of primitive communism were combined by early anthropologists in the image of the horde, living internally in a state of perfect communism, externally in a state of war against everyone. During the first quarter of the present century, good ethnographic fieldwork resulted in a different picture of early man. Ethnographers recognized the significance of the individual, of his rights and obligations in society, and of the prevalence of the rule of reciprocity.

If we simply had to inquire whether rules of reciprocity are found in every society, we would merely have to collect a number of ethnographies, handbooks, and essays supplying the desired documentation. However, there are more pressing problems. Although we do indeed find reciprocity everywhere, we never find a society where complete, balanced reciprocity prevails throughout. It is not only that the rule is often ignored by individual members of the group (disobedience is the fate of any rule) but that time and again the rule of reciprocity is obscured, curtailed, or even overruled by publicly recognized dictates (also rules!) of hierarchy, competition, power, charity, and communality – to mention only the more obvious ones. This raises questions with regard to the general validity of the rule of reciprocity. On the one hand we must consider reciprocity as rooted in the human condition; on the other, we must examine the impact of deviations on social cohesion. These are problems that cannot be solved by philosophical argument alone; they must be cleared up by interrogating the data presented by ethnography, by inquiring into the social and economic relations pertaining to simple societies. We may expect that the causes of the deviations from the golden rule of reciprocity are more easily observable in primitive than in modern civilization, where the network of interpersonal relations is covered by thick layers of legal regulations and social machinery.

Rules of reciprocity and of reciprocal behavior were reported by many early ethnographers, but the term reciprocity was rarely used. Edward Westermarck in his *Origin and Development of the Moral Ideas* (1906/08) spoke of retributive emotions[1]. Other observers confined themselves simply to reporting the relevant facts, as did W. H. R. Rivers in his contributions on kinship to the *Reports of the Cambridge Anthropological Expedition to Torres Straits* (1905 pp. 144 ff.; 1908 pp. 100 f.). A wealth of material, derived from the Melanesian and the North American areas, was available long before its importance to a better understanding of the basis of social coherence was recognized. Bronislaw Malinowski (1922, 1926) was the first who realized the significance of reciprocal relations and reciprocity generally for the social life and cohesion of primitive society, a discovery made during his fieldwork in the Trobriand Islands. In his early works, written while he was still untrammeled by a utilitarian functionalism[2], he framed the rule of reciprocity in the broad perspective of the whole field of interpersonal relations, that is, not only social and economic relations, but those involved in the administration of justice as well. Reciprocity has since remained an important topic in anthropological theory.

[1] Works quoted in the text are referred to by the date of first appearance. For the edition actually used the bibliography should be consulted. Thus I refer in the text to *Les Structures élémentaires de la Parenté* as Lévi-Strauss 1949, though quotations and references are from the 2nd edition of 1967.

[2] Although Malinowski uses the term function in different ways, the emphasis ordinarily is on the ability of a cultural institution to serve the vital needs of the community or its members. He rarely uses the term to indicate the relation prevailing between two sets of variables.

In the following sections we first present the facts and views brought up by a small number of scholars: Bronislaw Malinowski, Marcel Mauss, Claude Lévi-Strauss and Marshall Sahlins. We then turn to the problems of unbalanced reciprocity that, in the end, will lead us to the foundations of the rule of reciprocity in the human condition, and to the limitations set by this condition to the application of the rule in social life. The theoretical views developed in the course of this exposition will be tested in a section devoted to reciprocity in the administration of justice, a subject that has to be dealt with separately because of its specific nature. In conclusion we finally evaluate the role and effect of gift and trade – the prominent forms of reciprocal exchange – as models for social exchange in modern civilization.

2 *The Work of Bronislaw Malinowski*

It is the fashion today to let the praise of Malinowski as a great ethnographer be followed by the comment that he was a poor theoretician. Although this is true enough of the older Malinowski, it is unjust with regard to the author of *The Argonauts of the Western Pacific* (1922) and of its theoretical supplement, *Crime and Custom in savage Society* (1926). Rereading *The Argonauts* after so many years (I read it for the first time in 1929 and, though I consulted if often enough, I did not reread it as a whole until recently) I was impressed by the unfaded freshness of the argument and the analytic depth of the description. It captures all the unmistakable fragrance of Oceanic island life. The most attractive quality of the book is that we meet individuals, each a personality with his own peculiar virtues and vices, each living according to the rules where it suits him or where he cannot easily escape from doing so, and evading them when it is profitable to disobey and sanctions are not expected. It is, of course, what we expect of an ethnographic description today, but in 1922 it was new. Earlier ethnographers had always been more interested in rules and institutions than in the ways the people lived up to them. Primitive people were supposed simply to comply with their rules.

In *The Argonauts* and subsequent works, Malinowski reviews comprehensively the network of rights and obligations pertaining to the various roles and statuses of the individual. He tells us of the rights of the owner of a fishing-canoe and of his obligations to the men who assisted him in its construction, of the rights and duties obtaining between husband and wife, mother's brother and sister's son, wife's brother and sister's husband, and so on. Every role and function entails a variety of associated rights and obligations. The author himself drew up a full list of those that are of specific interest to us here, such as the various kinds of gifts, payments, and commercial transactions (Malinowski 1922 pp. 177 ff.). We follow this list because it is a fair illustration of the wide network of exchange relationships and a good introduction to the problems of balance and imbalance in reciprocal relations.

The first category mentioned is that of 'pure gifts', such as the presents a husband makes to his wife, or a father to his son. The term 'pure gift' is an unfortunate one, and Malinowski, realizing that there is always some sort of obligation connected with any gift, withdrew the term in *Crime and Custom* (pp. 40 ff.). In the latter work he included the gifts once called 'pure' in the very complex system of give-and-

15

take that embraces 'the whole system of gifts, duties, and mutual benefits exchanged between the husband on one hand, wife, children and the wife's brother on the other' (1926 p. 41), a system in which, according to the author, in the long run, the mutual services balance. Earlier and independently, M. Mauss had arrived at a similar conclusion. These gifts are neither free nor really disinterested. 'Mostly they are already return-gifts or services performed not only to pay for services and objects but also in view of maintaining a profitable relation' (Mauss 1924 p. 268)[3]. In their denial of the occurrence of free gifts the authors are, of course, perfectly right, but they would have done better to place them in the special category of the give-and-take that prevails in the continuous inter-action among the members of small groups, in which relations are of a more or less affectionate character. In addition, Malinowski errs when he contends that, in the long run, these mutual services balance. They do not. These small family groups are tolerant of the young, the weak, the infirm, and, often, even the dull. The weaker members are protected and helped by the stronger, the most obvious case being that of the children. It is only in exceptional cases that children even the balance for the parental care they received. And Malinowski further confuses the picture by including here the relations between a husband and his wife's brother, which, in the Trobriand Islands, are clearly unbalanced and also partly formal. On the other hand,

[3] Here and in other quotations from the French I give my own translation. The English translation of the *Essai sur le Don* at my disposal, the one by Cunnison (1966), is so inaccurate that it deterred me from using translations that I did not closely compare to the original. I did so with Cunnison's *Gift* and soon found out that Evans-Pritchard, who honored it with a laudative introduction, cannot possibly have done the same.

Mauss misses the point by associating these relationships with 'profitable relations'. The relationships may, in some cases, be profitable, but this is not a necessary characteristic.

The second category of gifts is that of 'payments, repaid irregularly and without strict equivalence' (Malinowski 1922 p. 180). Here belong the voluminous food-gifts annually brought by a brother to his sister's husband who, in this matrilineal society, takes care of his own wife and her brother's future heirs. The brother also assists his sister's husband whenever summoned by the latter to partake in some communal work. The return-gifts presented in acknowledgement of these gifts and services are 'not equivalent and regular, but spasmodic and smaller in value' (p. 150). The tributes given by vassal village communities to a chief and usually repaid by small counter-gifts, and the contributions given to a kinsman who has to make a mortuary distribution also belong to this class. The latter, too, may be repaid, but a strict balance is lacking. If, ultimately, there is a balance, it is a societal one of a statistical nature. The man who pays gifts and services to his sister's husband receives similar ones from his wife's brother. And those to whom he contributes a share in the mortuary distributions they have to make, will assist him when he is in similar straits. Finally, the chief repays the tribute offered to him by making big distributions of food on festive occasions, and he serves the community daily by organizing its communal affairs.

A third category in Malinowski's list of rights and duties is that of services rendered by the garden-magician (the term garden-priest would have been more appropriate), the medecine-man, the sorcerer, and the assistant in funeral ceremonies. The rewards are equivalent to the pains taken by the performers. Malinowski includes in this category also the small presents given by the male lover to his female partner in recognition of the pleasure enjoyed. Here he follows native usage, which classifies them all as *magula*, that is repayment, equivalent. The equivalence is, of course, a matter of native evaluation; it is extremely difficult to uncover the norms underlying the consensus that reward and service are equivalent.

A similar difficulty prevails in the fourth category, that of 'gifts returned in economically equivalent form' (1922 p. 184), such as those made in return for the lease of a garden plot, the gifts exchanged between friends, or those interchanged at the presentation of a new canoe. We may also include here Malinowski's fifth category, the payments made for the acquisition of magic or dances. They all have in common that service and payment, gift and countergift, are incommensurable and that their equivalence is a matter of standardized norms.

A more specific category is the sixth, that of ceremonial barter with deferred payment. There are two forms, *wasi* and *kula*. The former is the ceremonial exchange of fish for tubers that takes place between a coastal and an inland community, in which the quantities are standardized by tradition. The custom has a solid background in economic reality; the inlanders always have plenty of tubers but lack in fish, the coastal people have plenty of fish and are short of vegetable food. The exchange resembles ordinary barter but differs from it in form, since everyone in the two exchanging villages has his own special exchange-partner. There is no bargaining in this exchange; the visiting group brings its gifts, and each deposits his share in front of his partner's house, thus inviting him to make his return-gift. The invitation cannot be rejected. If tubers have been brought by the inlanders, their partners organize a fishing party as soon as the weather allows, and notify their friends that they can come to the beach to receive the fish straight from aboard the returning canoes.

The other form of ceremonial exchange is the famous *kula*, the exchange of armlets composed of two half-circles made of a big conic shell (*mwali*) for long strings of polished *spondylus* shells (*soulava*). Each participant has his own partners, some nearby in his own or adjoining districts, some overseas and far off. *Mwali* and *soulava* are highly esteemed valuables; they bear proper names, and just like our jewels, they are not all of equal worth, some of them being of much greater value than others. They may not be kept for long but must be offered in exchange to a partner who lives in a direction fixed by tradition. As *mwali* have to be exchanged for *soulava*, the *soulava* always travel clockwise, and the *mwali* counter-clockwise, thus connecting the Trobriand Islands in a huge ring of intertribal relations with the Woodlark- and Laughlan Islands to the east, and the Amphletts and Dobu to the south. There is no bargaining or asking in this exchange; the receiver has to wait for what in time his partner will give in return. Although the gift-giving is a public act that is publicly performed, it is bad form to pay attention to the object at the moment it is given, unless the donor is of high rank and the receiver is not. In such a case the receiver will accept the gift from the chief's hands with a token of reverence; otherwise, a boy will be summoned to pick up the object to carry it off. Giver and receiver display an indifference that veils their real feelings. The more genuine of the two is the donor; contemptuously throwing down the object in front of his partner's feet, he betrays his disinclination to part with the valuable object. At the same time, the rules of procedure help to keep things formal. The receiver will afterwards inspect the object meticulously but, if disappointed because the gift does not really equal the object for which it is a return-gift, he will not openly protest. He will confine himself to complaining to everyone else that the giver is mean in the *kula*. To be 'mean in the *kula*' is fatal for one's status and future position in the *kula*, and everyone who has to make a return-gift knows this. The natives put all their pride in a good reputation in the *kula*, and this is what keeps things going.

Finally there is trade pure and simple (*gimwali*). It is carried on, among other instances, between the people of the poor and low-status inland communities of the Kuboma-district and those of the prosperous villages on the coast and in the more fertile agricultural districts. Usually the former bring their wares (wooden dishes, combs, limepots, armlets, and baskets) to their customers, sitting down in groups and displaying their manufacture, saying, for example: 'You have plenty of coco-nuts, and we have none. We have made fine wooden dishes. This one is worth forty nuts, and some betel-nut, and some betel-pepper' (Malinowski 1922 p. 189). Haggling follows until a bargain is struck and the price is paid. A similar trade is carried on between inland villages and fishing communities, which do not stand in a traditional *wasi*-relation to each other. *Gimwali* is definitely differentiated from other forms of exchange. 'Scornfully criticizing bad conduct in Kula, or an improper manner of giving gifts, a native will say that 'it was done like a *gimwali*' ' (*ibid.*).

Although of another order than ceremonial and generalized exchange, *gimwali* is by no means of small importance. J. P. Singh Uberoi points out that it is the obvious means for the acquisition of goods that cannot be obtained otherwise (1962 pp. 148 ff.). The big *kula*-expeditions always go combined with *gimwali*, in which the visiting party brings trade-goods for barter with local products. There is one restriction; *kula*-partners cannot make *gimwali* with one another. They must barter with people to whom they are not committed by a ceremonial bond. Furthermore, upon the arrival of the visiting party no bartering can take place before a first ceremonial gift has been made, Malinowski did not pay much attention to this feature, but it is interesting enough to give it some further thought.

When preparing an overseas *kula*-expedition the people of Sinaketa (a southern district of the main island of the Trobriands) first pay a ceremonial visit to the northern districts, an occasion that is celebrated with an exchange of presents. The natives of Kuboma, the poor industrial district, avail themselves of the occasion and come to the coast to sell their products to the Sinaketans, who need these for their *gimwali* with the people of their *kula*-partners overseas (Malinowski 1922 p. 165). Thus, trade is performed under the umbrella of a ceremony. This is not always the case. We noted that the Kubomans can come to the more prosperous villages to offer their merchandise at any time. Reversely, people who need some of the objects manufactured in Kuboma will go there to purchase them. It is of interest, however, that Malinowski adds that people of rank will do so by giving an initial gift, expecting repayment, whereas others just go and barter (1922 p. 89). Apparently, barter depends upon either a ceremonial occasion, or on some form of pre-existing social contact, often a very weak form of contact. We shall return to this point later.

The exchange of goods and services in the Trobriand Islands reveals that the social fabric is woven of many strands of rights and obligations, some of them strictly reciprocal, some mildly so, and others unbalanced. Ceremonial exchange consolidates connections between men of wealth living in nearby or widely separated communities. Affinal relations are cemented by a strict system of presents and services so that a woman's brother becomes the provider and helper of his sister's household, a position that needs not be oppressive if his own wife has brothers who provide for him. Actually, the system creates differences of all sorts, a single girl with two or more brothers being a desirable match and a brotherless girl a poor one. Moreover, a man with two sisters, of whom one is married to a commoner and the other to a chief, will offer a greater harvest-gift to his noble brother-in-law than to the other. There is reciprocity in all relations, but its repeated lack of balance is obvious.

3 *Marcel Mauss on the Gift*

The functionalist Malinowski remained satisfied with the conclusion that reciprocity has a useful function because it creates a huge network of rights and obligations that generates social cohesion. The question of why people everywhere and always accept this useful, and even profitable, rule of reciprocity apparently never occurred to him. Had he entertained any doubts, he could hardly have failed to be perplexed by the universality of mankind's adherence to a useful rule, a fact uncommon enough to justify an additional analysis of the procedures of give-and-take, an analysis that could only have increased his doubts. In fact, a really rigid application of the rule of reciprocity sometimes can be as harmful to social relations as its more graded use often is beneficent.

To Marcel Mauss reciprocity was anything but a matter of course. His initial concern was with the contract and the historical development of that remarkable institution that enables two people to enter into mutual obligations in such manner as to make sure that the law (that is, society) will watch and, if necessary, enforce the faithful fulfilment of their agreement. In a contract two people pledge themselves to a 'prestation' and a 'counter-prestation', that is, to a service or a deliverance to be reciprocated by a service or deliverance in return. The gift, which is always followed by a countergift, presented itself as an intriguing prototype of the contract, the return-gift being as obligatory as the fulfilment of a contract. The only difference (one which never got the attention that it deserves!) is that contracts need the protection of law, and gifts do not.

Starting from the problem of the contract, Mauss situated his *Essai sur le Don* (1924) in the perspective of Émile Durkheim's *De la Division du Travail Social* (1893). Here Durkheim had argued that social evolution begins with the horde, in which an almost complete similarity of opinion generates strong feelings of togetherness and solidarity among its members. This emotion-based 'mechanic' solidarity evolves toward the 'organic' solidarity of societies in which specialization and division of labor create a state of mutual dependence among the members. Historical development thus combines the progressive importance of the individual and of individual decisions with a steady increase in the number and weight of binding relations. In other words, the development of the contract and the legal recognition of individual contractual agreements, parallels social evolution. When the problem of the contract was taken up again by Durkheim's successors, the fieldwork of ethnographers like Franz Boas, Malinowski, and others had already seriously impaired the point of departure of Durkheim's theory, his notion of primitive society as one in which undifferentiated individuals live in a state of communism and communalism. In *La Foi Jurée* (1922), a book on the history of the contract that appeared only two years earlier than the *Essai sur le Don*, Mauss' lifelong friend and collaborator, Georges Davy, still propounds the evolutionist viewpoint, but Mauss steers a freer course. He does not indulge in speculations upon early man, and he refers only in passing to Durkheim's thesis, *viz.* when he calls exchange 'the social division of labor itself' (Mauss 1924 p. 148). Instead, he applies himself straightaway to the available data on socioeconomic relations among Northwestern American Indians and Melanesians to study the gift, which in these and other societies is always reciprocated. What is the rule of law and interest that requires that a gift received is obligatorily reciprocated? What power is at work in the object given that causes the beneficiary to render something in return? (*loc. cit.*).

The exchange of goods and valuables by means of the gift is not the simple affair one might be inclined to guess:

'In the first place it is not individuals, it is collectivities who mutually commit themselves, who exchange and pledge themselves; the persons present at contracting are moral persons: clans, tribes, families who defy and confront each other, either in groups while opposing each other on the spot, or by the intermediary of their chiefs, or in both ways combined. Moreover, what they exchange are not exclusively goods and valuables, personal and real property, objects which are economically useful. Before all, these are courtesies, banquets, rites, military assistance, women, children, dances, feasts, fairs in which the market is but one of the elements and the circulation of wealth only one of the ends of a contract which is far more permanent' (Mauss 1924 p. 151).

We note the emphasis on the collective nature of these transactions that reminds us of Durkheim's theory of the *Division du Travail Social*. Nevertheless, the data fully justify the description of what Mauss calls 'total prestations' (services and deliverances), transactions in which not simply individuals, but whole groups are involved and the cooperation of families, clans, and even moieties is a must. The gifts are presented as voluntarily given, and yet they are rigorously obligatory, and the transactions themselves include all the diverse aspects of tribal life. The ideal type of these transactions is the *potlatch*, the ceremony of total exchange among the coastal tribes of British Columbia. The generosity displayed in the exchange is overwhelming, exhausting the total resources of the hosts and occasionally of their guests as well. This generosity, however, is far from genuine. Rather, it is combined with a definitely antagonistic trait that, in the North American potlatch, comes dangerously close to warfare. The big intertribal potlatch is more a war than a contest. One party tries to outdo the other with gifts of food, blankets, valuables, and so on, the ultimate aim being the humiliation of the party that has nothing left to give in return. Cases have been reported in which the parties concerned competed in the destruction of heirlooms, notably the highly prized copper plates that constitute the most important form of traditional wealth. In this contest for status and prestige the gift is used as a weapon. It has the power to humiliate, a power deriving from the principle that the superior gives more than the inferior. In this context, Mauss reminds us of the etymology of the word gift which, in the Germanic languages, has, among others, the connotation of poison (see Oxford English Dict., v. *gift*). There is ample reason for such a reminder; modern man, too, mixes an element of competition in his feasts. A party is followed by a return-party because we feel obliged (if we speak German) 'uns zu revanchieren', that is, to give (ourselves) a revenge (Mauss 1924 p. 153). We feel obliged: we wonder what there is in the thing given that urges the receiver to reciprocate.

Mauss gives a remarkable answer that is hardly an answer at all. Early in his essay, he cites a Maori statement that the *hau* (a kind of innate supernatural power) of a personal property goes along with it when it is given away, urging the receiver to reciprocate lest the *hau* of the property make him ill and kill him (pp. 158 f.). The given object is not just a thing; something of the giver travels along with it. Lévi-Strauss was, of course, perfectly right when he noted that the Maori statement does not explain anything. It is just another theory, in this case a native theory (*in* Mauss 1950 p. XXXIX). As a native theory, it is a strong affirmation of the binding effect of the gift, and Mauss, pursuing his argument, presents overwhelmingly rich evidence that everywhere we are confronted with three obligations: the one to give, to accept, and to return. The erudition of the author is impressive, the argument commanding, and the commentary clear and persuasive. Exchange binds groups and individuals, and the circulation of goods can be identified with a circulation of rights and individuals. The facts demonstrate 'that the principle of gift-exchange must have belonged to societies that have passed beyond the phase of 'total prestation'[4] but have not yet arrived at the stage of the pure, individual contract, at the sale proper, and above all at the notion of price expressed in weighed and coined money' (Mauss 1924 p. 227).

The author pursues the historical perspective in an analysis of Roman, Hindu, and Germanic law, demonstrating how much of this same spirit can still be traced in their archaic institutions, winding up his historical exposition with a curious case borrowed from Chinese law. Up to the time of the *Essai* a man who sold one of his goods, even if movable, retained the right during all his life to weep over it. It is somewhat like a right of pursuit, bearing witness to the archaic notion that a thing is not just a thing, but has ineffaceable connections with its original owner.

Little attention is paid to the evolution of the notions of buying and selling. The trend of the argument is clearly that pure sale is a latecomer in economic history and, to an extent, a contravening development as well, because it is evident that social relations have become looser concurrently. Nevertheless, Mauss does not give up hope that in the long run the atomizing effects of modern economic exchange will be overcome. In his conclusions (notably the 'moral conclusions' but the argument returns in his 'Conclusions de sociologie et d'économie politique') the author hails the rising tide of social insurance and welfare as a

---

[4] The phase of total prestation is the same as that of Durkheim's mechanic solidarity, in which everyone is like everyone else, and in which the action of each individual necessarily involves the group.

definite symptom of the restoration of the personal ties uniting employers and workers as well as sellers and buyers.

Our comment on the essay as a whole must begin by admitting that the author gave undeniable evidence of the comprehensive role played by the gift in archaic societies, a role many times more important than the one it plays in modern civilization. On the other hand, the developmental emphasis prevented him from giving due attention to the presence of trade pure and simple even in very slightly differentiated cultures, a point to which we shall return in a later section.

A curious trait of the *Essai* is its emphasis on the potlatch. In the treatise, this institution of the Kwakiutl and adjacent tribes who inhabit the coast of Vancouver, grows into a generic concept, covering exchange ceremonies of a comprehensive ('total') nature all over the world. Personally, I have my reservations on this point because the Kwakiutl potlatch is a rather specific form with a far stronger bias towards strife and aggression than exists in the Melanesian, or any other, area. On the other hand, it must be admitted that the potlatch is a highly instructive form of exchange, just because it exaggerates some of the most interesting aspects of gift-giving. One of these has been exposed by Marshall Sahlins (1968), who refers to Hobbes and the Hobbesian war of all against everyone as the ultimate background of Mauss' developmental philosophy, a surprising fact because in other respects Mauss was more inclined to follow Rousseau. Yet, Hobbesian strife is present in the potlatch, which continues the perennial war between the ever-hostile clans with means that prevent them from destroying each other and compel them to cooperate within limits. In a way, says Sahlins, the potlatch *is* the social contract, not the one that either Hobbes or Rousseau had in mind, but the one that, incorporated in the gift, unites parties who otherwise would destroy each other. It is the answer to the old choice formulated by E. B. Tylor, the one between being married out or being killed out (Tylor 1889). The fact that marrying out is the oldest prototype of the contract, had already been recognized by Davy (1922 p. 83).

Sahlins' interpretation, stimulating though it is, should not be stressed too much, lest we get lost in conjectural history. Another interpretation (which does not exclude the former but lays another emphasis) comes closer to the problems of inequality that were raised by Rousseau. It is the direct relationship that exists between the magnificence of gift and counter-gift on the one hand and the social positions of the respective givers on the other. He who gives most is highest in status, thus gifts can be used as weapons in a contest for status. Acknowledged inequalities permit a father to give 'freely' to his son, or a master to his servant without in either case insulting the admittedly inferior party. There is nothing that affirms so strongly the correlation between balanced reciprocity and equality as exactly this. Unequal status generates unbalanced reciprocity, and balanced reciprocity suggests social equality. Balanced reciprocity thus becomes the hallmark of equality. Again, this is, like Sahlins' comment, not an interpretation explicitly given by Mauss himself, but one implicit in his work. We shall have to come back to it later. For the moment, we confine ourselves to stating that Mauss presented the facts without solving the problem.

4 *Claude Lévi-Strauss on the Structures of Reciprocity and Gift-exchange*

The publication of *The Argonauts* and the *Essai* marked the beginning of a period of intensive field-work in which exchange relations received the full share of the ethnographers' attention. Malinowski's example and the new standards it set for fieldwork had an inspiring effect. Malinowski's view that reciprocity is a main rule for interpersonal transactions in every society was amply confirmed. Cases of balanced (and unbalanced) reciprocity were reported from everywhere. A satisfactory review of these ethnographies can be found in Sahlins' essay *On the Sociology of primitive Exchange* (1965). More conducive to our present purpose is a short examination of the contributions of Claude Lévi-Strauss to the study of reciprocity.

Until the appearance of the latter's *Elementary Structures of Kinship* in 1949, anthropologists had rarely shown more than a transient interest in the basic problems of reciprocity. Malinowski's view that the useful function of reciprocity explains its universal acceptance as a rule was fairly generally followed, in spite of the notorious fact that universality cannot be explained on the basis of usefulness. The casual imbalance of reciprocity, another problem that functionalism cannot easily solve, was not recognized as a problem before 1960 (see Gouldner 1960). The line of thought developed by Mauss had not been pursued either, developmental and evolutionist problems being fairly unpopular during those years when the processes of the actual functioning of a society monopolized the studies of anthropologists. Yet the problem raised by Mauss was one of great interest. Fundamentally it was the problem of why *pacta sunt servanda* – why pacts should be kept. The ready acceptance of the rule in the *mores* of gift-exchange promised the solution of an important problem of moral and legal philosophy. If the fundamental rule of the contract is obeyed in such manifestly voluntary transactions as gift-exchanges in which the size and nature of the return-gift are left to the discretion of the beneficiary, then it stands to reason that reciprocity is a binding obligation in contracts stipulating in detail the obligations agreed upon by both parties. But then, why should contracts be more explicitly protected by law than gift-exchange? Unfortunately, Mauss had not succeeded in giving a proper explanation of the obedience to the rules that he had described so well, nor had he pursued his analysis far enough to disclose the conflicting trends separating the gift from the contract.

Lévi-Strauss, in spite of his reservations regarding the validity granted by Mauss to the Maori explanation of the gift as the bearer of *hau*, closely associated himself with Mauss' other views. The survey of the principal implications of gift-exchange and reciprocity in the chapters 5 and 7 of *The Elementary Structures*, can be characterized as a lucid and concise summary of the *Essai sur le Don*. Yet, it is more than this; it also is an improvement on it on more than one point.

Thus, Lévi-Strauss argues that gift-exchange is not essentially or even primarily geared to the acquisition of benefits or economic advantages, but to ends of a more social nature, such as power, the winning of sympathy, status, or emotion (Lévi-Strauss 1949 p. 63). This is true whether the exchange is of the potlatch type that involves the cooperation of broad sections of society in activities including several aspects of community life, or of the more modest type

31

that constitutes a simple exchange between affines on the occasion of such a commonplace event as a birth. We should further include among the social objectives of gift-exchange the consolidation of good relations, communication being the most central aim of human interaction in structuralist theory. In fact, the exchange often does not serve any economic purpose at all. Then it is as if the exchange has its end in itself, for instance when the goods exchanged are perfectly identical, a package of cooked food for an identical package, a reindeer for a reindeer, and so on (*ibid.*).

Lévi-Strauss' short review distinguishes between trade and gift-exchange. Although he does not enter deeper into the subject, the data provided arouse the expectation that there might be good sense in pursuing the ins and outs of the difference. A good case is that of the story told of Amundsen, the arctic explorer. Amundsen found that his own generous return-gifts to the presents made to him by the Eskimo had persuaded the latter that it was to their advantage to offer their merchandise not for sale, but as gifts, because the return-gifts were richer than what they could hope for in the way of commercial barter. 'He soon had to refuse every present and to revert to commerce properly speaking' (1949 p. 64). Apparently, the Eskimo distinguish trade from gift-exchange as definitely as the Trobrianders do.

The author's comment on the role of gift-exchange in the everyday life of our own society is illuminating. He tells the story of two men, strangers to each other, who face each other at a small table in a cheap restaurant somewhere in the south of France where a minuscule bottle of poor wine is part of everyone's menu. There they sit, both members of a culture that discourages chatting with a perfect stranger, yet each too close to the other to ignore his presence. When the meal is served, one of them solves the difficulty. He opens his small bottle and empties it into the other man's glass, a courtesy that is promptly reciprocated. They now can, and do, talk (1949 p. 69).

In a first summary of the principles to which he appeals in the introductory part of his *Elementary Structures* Lévi-Strauss mentions three mental structures universally in force: the claim of the rule as a rule (that is, the recognition of the validity of rules), the notion of reciprocity, and the synthetic character of the gift (1949 p. 98). We abstain from comment on the first of these 'structures' and concentrate on the other two. Reciprocity and gift-exchange are kept separate from each other, and rightly so, because reciprocity covers a wider range than the exchange of gifts. Reciprocity is described as 'the most immediate form under which the opposition between the I and the other can be integrated' (p. 98). To the uninitiated in structuralism the statement must seem confusing. Is not the confrontation between the I and the other the empirical basis of all reciprocity? In a way it is, and in the comment given by Lévi-Strauss in the subsequent pages the empiricist gets his full share. The author refers to the study made by Susan Isaacs of the behavior of young infants, of their egoism, their conflicts, their love and hatred, and how they discover that the only way to carry on with each other is by submitting to the rules of reciprocity and equality. Reading these pages the empiricist is inclined to exclaim: 'It is exactly as I have always said; the experience of one person meeting the other impresses upon both of them the notion of reciprocity'. The empiricist is wrong. If the structure, or the trend, of the unconscious did not lead everyone to interpret the experience of confrontation in terms of reciprocity, people would not accept it universally as the natural answer. Some might have chosen a rule of submission, others one of dominance, but they all decide for reciprocity and equality. Such unanimity is unintelligible unless we accept that a common structure or trend of the mind moulds their reactions toward a common conclusion[5].

The argument is a strong one. The rule of reciprocity has an inevitability that strongly suggests a foundation in the human mind or condition. However, this does not solve our problems; it only places them in a wider context. Unfortunately, this context is more obscured than elucidated by Lévi-Strauss' statement that reciprocity and the gift are mental structures, a formulation that suggests that they are more or less autonomous trends, similar to a drive or an instinct. Now this is most certainly not what Lévi-Strauss had in mind. What he really meant is that the human mind *as a whole* is so structured that, given certain conditions, the notion of reciprocity and the synthetic character of the gift are its necessary products. This raises the question of what these necessary conditions are, a question not further examined by Lévi-Strauss who had other, more pressing problems. He sought to determine the effect on the structures of kinship of the concurrence of the claim of the rule as a rule, of reciprocity, and of the implications of the gift. In this context he could afford to use these as 'fundamental data of mental reality from which to start every effort at explanation' (1949 p. 158). Our task is different. We know that the rule of reciprocity, seemingly one of pure logic, is liable to a disquieting number of ex-

[5] But note that the recognition of a rule does not imply obedience!

ceptions. We must ascertain the conditions that determine whether the rule shall be applied or modified, whether reciprocity shall be balanced, unbalanced, or even ignored. Gift-exchange raises other, equally intriguing problems. It is a form of exchange that, according to the lucid definition of Lévi-Strauss, is characterized by 'the fact that the agreed transfer of a value from one individual to another changes the two into partners and adds a new quality to the value transferred' (1949 p. 98). In this the gift differs widely from another common form of exchange, the sales transaction. Where the gift makes partners whose partnership endures, the sales transaction is performed between parties who afterwards disperse without any further obligation to each other. Why does one form of exchange bind and the other not? For an answer to these questions we shall have to return to an examination of the diversity of the forms of exchange in social life and to the situations and motives that are relevant to the various infractions of the rule of reciprocity.

5 Marshall D. Sahlins on Types of Reciprocity

Reciprocity has become an important topic of discussion in modern anthropology. A review of the extensive literature would entangle us in a controversy about details that would rather blur than clarify the central problems. We shall therefore confine ourselves to Marshall Sahlins' essay On the Sociology of Primitive Exchange (1965), one of the major studies of more recent years. Based upon an extensive collection of well-analyzed data from simple cultures, it raises questions of focal interest that are connected with the balance of exchange.

Sahlins first introduces a new distinction, that discriminates between economic transactions of the reciprocal type, and those of the pooling, or redistribution, type. On closer inspection it turns out that the pooling or redistribution type is an alternative of the reciprocal type. A central authority is presupposed, a chief or a headman, who receives contributions (sometimes called tribute) from the members of the group, contributions that at a later date will be redistributed when a ceremony, a war, the preparation of a trade expedition, or succour in times of scarcity, induce the chief to display his generosity. From this point of view, the redistribution is an act of delayed reciprocity. The prestige that the chief derives from it is a compensation for his troubles in behalf of the community. The material benefit that the chief enjoys is not substantial. Since his prestige is a function of his generosity, a chief cannot afford to be mean. There cannot be real saving in an economy of ostentatious giving. Pooling 'is the complement of social unity' (Sahlins 1965 p. 141). It has its prototype in familial pooling of food, and thus pooling and redistribution can be defined as forms of generalized reciprocity (1965 pp. 141 ff., 147).

Generalized reciprocity introduces a second typology of forms, the typology dominating the body of the essay. Sahlins distinguishes among generalized reciprocity (defined as the solidary extreme), balanced reciprocity (the mid-point), and negative reciprocity (the unsociable extreme). The criteria refer to the supposed contributions made by each type to the social cohesion of the group or groups concerned. According to Sahlins the ideal type of generalized reciprocity is Malinowski's 'pure gift' (1965 p. 147), rather an unfortunate reference as Malinowski himself retracted

36

the term. Be that as it may, implied in Sahlins' use of the term are informal reciprocity, generosity, kinship dues, tributes to chiefs, and contributions to pooling activities. In generalized reciprocity, reciprocity is often weak, and of great benefit to the infirm and the destitute.

Sahlins notes that balanced reciprocity refers to direct exchange, although various forms of delayed requital should be included. Much buying and selling enter into this type of exchange, which also includes gift-exchange of a more formal, and always commensurate, nature. He adds that 'the material side of the transaction is at least as critical as the social' (1965 p. 148).

Negative reciprocity, finally, is 'the attempt to get something for nothing with impunity, the several forms of appropriation, transactions opened and conducted towards net utilitarian advantage. Indicative ethnographic data include 'haggling' or 'barter', 'gambling', 'chicanery', 'theft', and other varieties of seizure' (*ibid*).

There is a correlation between the three types and social distance. In the household generalized reciprocity prevails; in intratribal intercourse, balanced reciprocity; and in intertribal traffic, negative reciprocity. Overlappings, however, are numerous, and much of Sahlins' essay is devoted to the reasons for the overlaps. We shall not follow him in his often absorbing analyses. We only note that it is balanced reciprocity that, in his exposition, remains the most puzzling of all. On the one hand, the fact that accounts are squared can imply that a relationship is exhausted because there is no longer that 'shadow of indebtedness' that holds the participants together in generalized reciprocity. 'Balanced exchange may tend toward self-liquidation'.

On the other hand, there are as many cases of trust and confidence being built by 'a series of honorably balanced dealings between comparatively distant parties' (1965 p. 178).

Sahlins' typology does not lead to a clear-cut categorization of the relevant facts. Other typologies suffer from comparable shortcomings. One of the more obvious possibilities is a distinction between exchange for economic and for social reasons, a distinction made, among others, by Peter Blau (1967 pp. 88 ff.). Here the difficulty arises that almost every exchange has an economic as well as a social aspect, as is well demonstrated by the following statement made by Luc de Heusch with reference to marriage arrangements: 'The necessities of alliance and filiation mark a universal ideological structure, but the exchange, which is its regulatory principle, is already an economic reality in every respect' (De Heusch 1971 p. 102; Van Baal 1972 p. 122). In gift-exchange of the more formal kind, always a socially important transaction, the future acquisition of a substantial countergift is often anticipated, even to the extent that this can be one of the primary motives of the individual who gives an opening present. Sometimes the ultimate reason for the exchange seems purely economic. A good case is that of the already described *wasi*, the ceremonial barter of tubers for fish in the Trobriand Islands. On the other hand, an undoubtedly purely economic act such as *gimwali* often depends on the celebration of some ceremony. And Mauss suggested that pure trade might well have developed from gift-exchange.

It is evident that the direct application of our categories of 'social' and 'economic' on data borrowed from archaic and primitive cultures does not lead us much beyond the well-known fact that these fields of human action, so neatly discerned by us (though perhaps not as neatly as we think) are hopelessly entangled in primitive societies. But could we really expect anything different? Is it not an error of method to submit the forms of primitive life to a categorization of contents derived from our culture? Should we not start from more primitive forms? The Trobrianders, with their explicit distinction between *gimwali* and other kinds of exchange, present us with a workable instrument for further analysis. We have already found that among the Eskimo a similar distinction apparently is made, and the ethnographic evidence indicates that the distinction is widespread. We turn first to the Trobrianders for a possible solution to the problem of why exchange is sometimes balanced and sometimes not.

6 *Trade and Gift-exchange*

The difference between *gimwali* and the Trobriand forms of ceremonial exchange is the difference between trade and gift-giving. In gift-exchange goods are exchanged for the purpose of establishing or strengthening a relation between the persons who make the exchange. In trade the relations between those engaged are weak (*kula*-partners are not allowed to *gimwali* with each other) and the participants' aim is not to strengthen their mutual relations but to acquire one another's goods. Whereas the gift establishes or strengthens a bond, a sale exhausts the (weak) link between the traders; the act accomplished, the parties disperse without any future obligation toward each other. They need not meet again. Every buyer is free everywhere to go to another firm or shop the next time he is in need of a commodity. Even in the case of traders who deal regularly with each other (not uncommon in economically more advanced societies) the relationship remains commercial, distinct from the personal ties that may have developed in the course of prolonged contacts. But a gift-exchange obliges the givers to continue their relations and to behave not like individual parties, but as partners. Let us have a closer look at the details.

The ideal of trade is balanced reciprocity. Personal relations do not interfere with an objective evaluation of the goods offered for sale. Sahlins classified haggling as a form (admittedly an innocuous form) of negative reciprocity, thus suggesting that haggling involves an effort at undeserved profit. It often does, but this is no more than a side effect of a technique geared to the realization of strict equivalence. Fixed prices are a recent, Western development, and even then mostly in retail-trade, not on the international market. From time immemorial, trade has been associated with bargaining, a term to be preferred to haggling, which has a somewhat deprecatory connotation and is often too easily used by Europeans and Americans who are unskilled in the technique of bargaining. Forced to partake in bargaining when visiting an Eastern market, Westerners tend to spoil the game. Paying the demand price too quickly, they walk off with a well-founded sense of humiliation, feeling that they have been cheated, little realizing that the vendor feels the same way and accuses himself of silliness because he did not ask a higher price. Evidently, equality and balance are sadly lacking here, because this is not true trade. The Western bungler did not follow the rules of the game. Behaving as a stranger, he was treated as one. Imbalance, of course, can also be the result when one of the two trading parties holds a monopoly position, thus excluding the possibility of true bargaining[6]. Normally, bargaining is the technique for establishing an adequate price. This is as true of the New York Stock Exchange as it is of the Trobriand *gimwali*. Parties accustomed to the technique do not think it particularly difficult. They have little fear that they are being cheated. (For a discussion of the Javanese village market see Dewey 1962 pp. 73 f.). Bargaining aims at and results in fairly balanced exchange. It owes this result to the element of dispute that does not harmonize too well with close personal relations. The ban on carrying on *gimwali* with a *kula*-partner proves that the natives are well aware of this. A further examination of the facts may lead to interesting conclusions.

Earlier mention has been made of Uberoi's argument that trade is a far more important component of the big *kula*-expeditions than the superficial reader of Malinowski's description might guess. The accompanying *gimwali* supplies the islanders with a number of urgently needed commodities that cannot be acquired or produced locally (Uberoi 1962 p. 148). We found that trade is carried on under the umbrella of ceremony or between people who live in peace with each other without knowing each other too well. As traders require a situation permitting peaceful bar-

---

[6] The reader's attention is called to the many ambiguities involved in the term monopoly. Every trader who offers his ware disposes of some form of monopoly. Bargaining is the means of evaluating the relative weight of the competing monopolies. When all is said and done, this relative weight constitutes the ultimate ratio of all trade, since all ownership includes a form of monopoly.

gaining, such a situation, if failing, must be created. It does not present itself naturally, because traders are not usually closely related to each other. The occasion to trade, if it does not present itself by chance, must be purposively created. This is the situation among the Trobrianders, and similar conditions prevail elsewhere.

A good case is that of the *hiri*, the annual trading-expedition of the Motuans of Port Moresby to the Papuan Gulf. They bring their pottery on big rafts to the Gulf coast to barter for sago, starch obtained from the pith of a palm and an important nutrient in these parts. Bartering begins after the leaders of the expedition have exchanged gifts with their hosts (Seligman 1910 pp. 108 ff.). Once a kind of truce has been established, everyone can carry on his affairs.

The *hiri* is a rather exceptional affair, as is the *kula*. More commonplace is the institution of trade-friendship, which in New Guinea is well developed. Such friendships are very common among the mountaineers, and one of the better described cases is that of the Kuma. Trade-friends are like relatives; they exchange presents and help each other whenever possible. They guarantee their friends' safety and help them to acquire the commodities they are after. The procedure followed is one of a balanced exchange of gifts, not of bargaining. However, while he is travelling, the trader has an opportunity to enter into direct bargaining with passers-by or with any other people who have no special relations with him (Reay 1959 pp. 105 ff.). The trade-friendship is a mutual gift-relation that promotes opportunities for commercial barter. It is a fair guess, although one that requires additional critical examination of the relevant data, that the *kula*, this mysterious and even exalted form of gift-exchange, is essentially an overdeveloped form of institutionalized trade-friendship.

In economically more advanced societies we find markets, that is, institutionalized opportunities for barter between people who do not know each other personally. Peace within the precincts of the market is guaranteed by tradition and, if necessary, by the personnel attendant to it. Visitors are often forbidden to carry weapons. The institution of a new market is a matter of ceremony. The market has its regulations, and usually a small indemnity must be paid by the traders to the clerk of the market. The market is not necessarily open to every casual trader. In precolonial Indonesia a skipper, always a merchant himself, on arriving with his vessel in a Javanese or Sumatran port, would first wait upon the harbormaster to pay rights and duties. He would then pay homage (involving a sizable present) to the local prince. Only then was he admitted to the market to trade (Meilink-Roelofsz 1962 p. 43).Almost wherever we look, it is always the same picture: trade is transacted between relative strangers who are not tied to each other by special relations, who meet each other on special occasions or in special places where peace is assured. As trade is a matter of bargaining, it is always balanced, or at least meant to be balanced, and it is impersonal. It does not have, nor is it meant to have a unifying effect. Though persons meet and deal with each other, they are not interested in each other's person but in each other's goods. They are not partners but parties to each other. And, finally, trade has been found to exist everywhere, even in very primitive cultures. If in primitive society it is of small importance, that is because goods are few and material needs are underdeveloped, which, in turn, means that the relevant social conditions are underdeveloped too. Typically, in such a primitive situation, transactions take the form of silent trade, the perfect model for the peaceful barter of desired goods between parties who avoid every personal contact.

With the gift it is the other way round. The participants are not parties but, as Lévi-Strauss says, partners. Gift-exchange is an act in which the giver takes the receiver seriously, giving with his gift full value to the other's person. He recognizes the other's status and circumstances, and he expresses that what really counts is not gift or countergift, but the other one's person. The other can be a housemate, a personal friend, a cousin, or an affine; he can be older or younger, of higher or lower rank or an equal, a tribesman or a relative stranger, living in prosperity or in need, celebrating a feast or cast down by mourning. All of these factors necessarily affect the character of the gift as well as the way of presenting it. Housemates and close relatives rarely exchange gifts, and if they do, they usually do it informally. The common bond uniting them is so evident that they do not feel the need to affirm it explicitly. Among the members of small groups who really belong together, there is little opposition between ego and alter; they simply assist each other whenever necessary, without any other bookkeeping than of the inclination of each to mutuality. A defaulter in this respect will surely be called to order.

With more distant relations gift-exchange is more formal, as it certainly is between people who are relative strangers to each other. If of equal rank, strictly balanced reciprocity will be observed. If a recognized rank difference obtains, the superior tends to give more than the inferior is expected to return, just as parents usually give more to their children than the children will ever return. The principle has found a curious, we might say even an adverse application in the contest between rivals. It is essential that they exchange presents lest rivalry deteriorate into open hostility, which would lead not to a ranking of relations but to their ultimate dissolution. As long as rivals keep their competition well under control, the exchange of gifts between them will be of the strictly balanced kind. If competition gets the upper hand, the result is not open war, but a contest in which each rival publicly challenges the other to demonstrate his superiority by outdoing him in magnificence. As we have noted, the classical case is that of the Kwakiutl potlatch. It has gained greater notoriety than its exceptional character justifies. Even in the context of the rivalry and individual prowess favored in various Amerindian cultures, the big Kwakiutl potlatch is (in contrast to the ordinary smaller celebrations) a case of abortive exaggeration. Vying in generosity, the contestants mix the more friendly feelings expressed in their gift-giving with so much hostility and rivalry that the giving loses its unifying effect and degenerates into an instrument of civic destruction. At a certain stage the contest in gift-giving changes into a contest in the destruction of valuables. The gift disappears from the scene and a form of controlled warfare by means of calculated destruction takes its place.

The generalization of the term *potlatch* as a technical term for occasions of ceremonial gift-exchange of a total character has the disadvantage of overstressing the element of rivalry. Of course, rivalry easily slips in among the components of gift-exchange between groups that are not closely related. Self-preservation and assertion of status are important motives, but they are not usually permitted to overrule the fundamental aim, which is to achieve unison. Competitive food-exchange on a truly grandiose scale has been reported from various tribes in southern New Guinea. Among these tribes the rule prevailed that the loser in the contest had to be given an opportunity to make good for his deficiency by means of a return feast. The competitors saw to it that ultimately the quantities of food given by each party were equivalent. The aim was not strife but peace (cf. Landtman 1927 p. 395; Williams 1936 p. 234; Serpenti 1965 ch.6). The pursuit of prestige is not allowed to become more important than the pursuit of good relations. In unstratified societies like those of New Guinea, competitive giving is held in check by the requirements of social equality.

Stratified societies are different. Here competition is at home, the acquisition of wealth being one of the conditions for the achievement of rank. Kwakiutl society is a typical case, but its forms of wealth and competition are fairly unusual. Most stratified societies are found among cattle breeders, where livestock is the dominant form of wealth. The owner of an animal is sentimentally attached to it (for a good case see Evans-Pritchard 1940, ch. I). The animal is valuable to him and thus worth of being presented as a gift. It can produce new wealth but its durability is limited. Though value may increase with age (as it does with the buffalo in East Indonesian Flores, where long horns are highly appreciated), the animal is not allowed to die of old age. Livestock, like *kula*-articles, cannot be kept. The animals must be given away or sacrificed and consumed. The potlatch of stock-farming communities combines distribution with destruction in a socially more beneficent way than that of the Kwakiutl, permitting everyone to share in the distribution of meat. The conspicuous destruction of livestock is rarely combined with open rivalry. An occasion is usually not wilfully created by challenging an opponent, but awaited. Preferred occasions for demonstrating wealth and earning prestige are mourning feasts and marriages. One of the few cases of open competition that I know of is that of the competitive slaughtering of buffaloes by quarreling Sumbanese noblemen in East Indonesia. The litigants must be of comparable wealth. Onvlee makes mention of a relatively poor man who had been challenged to such an encounter. He brought a chicken to the meeting and quietly cut off its head, thus shaming the challenger for defying an unequal party (Onvlee 1973 p. 22).

The correlation between the size of a gift and the giver's status has more and brighter consequences than merely turning a gift into an instrument of competition. It is no mean thing that the rich should give more than the poor. In our culture where, since Rousseau, the wind of social equality has developed into a strong and steady gale, we think of social inequality as a wrong. In other cultures, differences are respected as pillars of the world order. In such societies, the rule that the rich give more than the poor and the knowledge that their prestige depends upon their generosity, turn the rich and the powerful into the patrons of the poor, and make them responsible for their weal or woe. Of course, this does not always work well, but where material culture is simple and conspicuous wealth strictly limited in scope, the differences between the standards of living of the poor and the rich are relatively small and are easier to bear than in more advanced societies where the rich have unlimited opportunities for squandering their wealth on egoistic ends. In simple societies a rich man's wealth is restricted to one or two commodities such as cattle, food, or shells, of which he has in abundance; nothing can be done with it except to give it away (see Mair 1936 p. 308 f.). In our present-day world, where, even in its remotest corners, everything can be converted into money and from money into the variegated forms of conspicuous wealth, this is no longer true, but the passing of the system should not prevent us from appreciating its beneficent aspects: the obligation to give and the direct proportion prevailing between the strength of the obligation and the owner's relative wealth[7].

There is one aspect of the gift that, so far, has not been discussed. The gift must please the recipient and also must be a token of the giver's appreciation of the receiver's person. This has its consequences. If it is a simple gift of food it must be tasty and good; if it is a more formal one it must be valuable. One cannot give away just anything; real giving is giving something valued by the giver himself. Here again the Trobriand *kula* is of interest. *Kula*-articles are genuine

[7] The principle is of specific importance in sacrifice. Anthropologists often expressed amazement that the gods usually receive only a minuscule portion of the animals sacrificed, the major portion – if not all of it – being distributed among the guests of the sacrificer. Sometimes it is as if the gods are cheated; offering a chicken, the sacrificer calls it a buffalo, and so on. Actually, there is not the slightest reason for amazement. Are not the gods infinitely rich and powerful? They only need a really small portion, not for food, but as a symbol of the intention of the sacrificer. Giving more would be preposterous and not in accordance with the immeasurable rank-difference. It is the intention which counts, the gesture of submission.

valuables, many times more expensive than the goods bartered at the associated *gimwali*. Besides being valuables, they are personal ornaments. Nothing could be more appropriate to express appreciation of another's person than ornaments with which the beneficiary can adorn himself. In our culture we still exchange wedding-rings, which are real valuables expressing a bond between the partners, in this case even a lifelong bond. All over the world we find that the most expensive, the really costly articles, are ornaments, whether they be feathers (princely gowns in Mexico and Hawaii were made of brightly colored feathers), or shells, jewels, golden rings or necklaces.

Malinowski, on his return from Melanesia, paid a visit to Edinburgh Castle where he viewed the crown jewels (Malinowski 1922 p. 88). Of incredible value, ugly and useless, the jewels strongly reminded him of the shell valuables of the Trobrianders, and with reason. The notion of value can hardly have originated in economically necessary barter. In primitive societies ignorant of a notion of money, barter is a direct exchange in which each party gives from what he has in plenty and is therefore of no specific use to him. He values the goods of the opposite party, not what he is going to give for them. The essence of bargaining is to discover what another is willing to give for the goods you offer.

With the gift it is different. Each must give what is valuable to himself, and there is no society so primitive that it has no valuables that can be exchanged as gifts. This is what changes the participants into partners and adds to the value of the goods exchanged (Lévi-Strauss 1949 p. 98). The intentions that go with the gift make it all the more valuable to the recipient. Although this is not the place to expatiate on the

origin of the notion of value, all the evidence points
in the direction of the gift[8].

7 *The Human Condition*

Our discussion of gift-exchange and trade has, in spite
of its rather rigmarole character, revealed a number of
remarkable ideal-typical differences that can be sum-
marized as follows:

TRADE	GIFT-EXCHANGE
Traders functionally each other's equals	Participants not always equals
Social relations weak, exhausted by completed exchange	Social relations strong, strengthened by completed exchange
Aims at the other one's goods	Aims at the other one's person
Goods exchanged usually lowly valued	Goods exchanged often highly valued
Strict reciprocity, balanced	Reciprocity not always balanced
No obligation to trade or to accept an offer	Obligation to give and to accept a gift
Contracts (trade-relations) protected by law	Gifts not protected by law
Trade does not bind participants	Gifts bind, turn participants into partners

[8] A few indications must suffice. One of the oldest forms of
money is kauri-shells. As such, they are in use in the mountains
of western New Guinea and in Africa. They were found in the
cave of Grimaldi, a species not deriving from the Mediterranean
but from the Indian Ocean (Perry 1923 pp. 457, 481). In New
Guinea they are used only partly as money, that is, as a standard
of value. They also are an indispensable part of the bride-price.
It is worth while to have a close look at these shells. If ever

Trade is a matter of simple logic. Parties are equals, unimpeded by intervening social relations, interested only in goods and their value, and free to offer, to accept, or to refuse as they like. Reciprocity is complete, balanced, and equal like the parties are. Trade is directed by a deliberate weighing of pros and cons, of free and conscious decisions.

It is the gift that raises problems. A gift offered cannot properly be refused as in trade, and in spite of the fact that the average value of a gift tends to exceed that of merchandise, reciprocity is not always balanced. Moreover, there is the obligation to give, an obligation that cannot be explained away by reducing it to the obligation to redistribute pooled goods, that is, to a form of delayed (or generalized) reciprocity. Of course, many of the distributions made by a chief are of this kind, and so are those made by the father or leader of the household. All of these redistributions are part of a continuous process of give-and-take in which reciprocity lacks the precision that is so characteristic of trade.

there was a symbol of the *vagina dentata*, it is the kauri-shell. Africans as well as Papuans, by cutting off the back of the shell, added substantially to the symbolic suggestion. Nothing could be more appropriate as a bride-price than these shells, certainly in the context of their respective marriage traditions. The shells are in the first place used as gifts, and only in the second place as money. With gold and silver it is not or, more exactly, was not very much different. They were used for the manufacture of ornaments, that is, of valuables, and only afterwards for the manufacture of coins, that is, for small quantities of a fixed value. Valuables other than precious metals cannot easily be divided into fixed quantities, but some shells are an exception, notably those that are small and available in sufficient, though limited quantities. Such a shell is the kauri-shell in inland areas.

51

To an extent, the hunter's obligation to distribute his catch can be considered as another example of generalized reciprocity. Here again a certain imbalance is evident; successful hunters are few, and the prestige they enjoy is not necessarily an adequate recompense for their troubles.

Another interesting feature is the obligation to give. Anyone who wishes to enter into a relationship with someone not a member of his group, has to begin by offering him a gift. Giving is obligatory also on the occasion of a funeral or a marriage, and in times of scarcity for those who are not short of food. Giving is an obligation that presses hardest on those who have more than others; a very fortunate fact perhaps, but why is this a general rule? And why is a gift so compelling that one cannot refuse it without insulting the giver, or neglect to give without insulting a potential receiver?

These are questions of a very general nature and an answer to them cannot possibly be a matter of special situations or cases. We must return to the fundamental conditions of human existence to understand what a gift means to a giver or a receiver. Elsewhere (Van Baal 1971 pp. 219 ff.) I have dwelled at some length on the dialectics of man's fundamental experience of himself, both as a part of his universe and as a subject separate from it. Man belongs to his universe and must participate in it, but he is conscious of himself as a subject apart from and even opposing his universe, capable of action according to his private wishes and preferences. He is and must be a self, but whatever the self wills or wishes, he must live with his universe; only this can give meaning to his life, can provide it with a defining frame. Yet, any time he takes cognizance of his situation he runs the risk of recognizing himself as an alienated subject, isolated from and lacking significant connection with his universe. Even primitive man knows what alienation is. The relatively high incidence of suicide confirms this. He too needs the affirmation that he really is part of his world. But the affirmation that is the product of intellectual reasoning discloses and increases man's alienation as a subject apart. Rather, he requires the affirmation implicit in the experience of feeling at home. He seeks the unreflective awareness of meaningful relations with the nature surrounding him, and with his fellow-men who share his world. Feelings are part of man's existence.

All his pride and self-consciousness do not prevent man from being a home-sick waif. A gift is more to him than simply a free meal. The gift is aimed at his person and represents an invitation to partnership. It confirms to the receiver that he is part of his universe, that others recognize him as such and wish to communicate with him. A gift is a real godsend; how could it be refused? The only circumstances under which it can be refused are that the giver is an enemy one wishes to hurt, or that one suspects a bribe. If the latter is the case, the situation requires cautious handling. To give an example: many colonial administrators found that an occasional gift presented to them by a local trader or contractor made difficult demands upon their tact: they could not accept the gift because they suspected a bribe, and they could not bluntly refuse it either, because the giver belonged to another culture in which different notions of decency prevailed which, within certain limits, ought to be respected.

However, a real gift is an invitation to partnership and is as wholeheartedly accepted as it is returned. Partnership is a dear thing to any man; it implies communication and this is why gift-exchange does not need protection by law as contracts do. Contracts are the result of bargaining, not, as in trade, bargaining on present goods, but over future deliverancies and services. There is nothing in such a trading transaction that can bind parties. They must either pledge a security or submit the fulfilment of their pact to the supervision of an authority who is willing to enforce the performance of their vows and capable of preventing chicanery. Parties to contracts are relative strangers to each other, with each intent on his own profit. To the contrary, the parties in gift-exchange become partners, and are willing to remain so. Their act is a friendly act, affirming their full participation in their universe.

Just as accepting and returning gifts are dictated by the inner need of communication and partnership, so is giving. Giving is the offering of one's self as a partner, and the confirmation of the giver's sincere participation in the receiver's troubles, needs, or happiness. This does not exclude the possibility that the giver's generosity is mixed up with ulterior motives of an egoistic nature. As a matter of fact, such is often the case, and it is unlikely that these ulterior motives escape the receiver's notice. Even so, there is comfort in the reflection: 'he has thought of me'.

The gift is such an important means of communication that its abuse for egoistic purposes that have only to do with the giver's private interests, is almost a matter of course. The receiver often is well aware of this, and will not speak of a gift, but of a bribe. He can do one of three things: refuse it, explaining to the giver why he cannot possibly accept; answer the gift with a return-present of equal value, an impossibility when the giver is rich and the receiver comparatively poor; or accept the gift and do as expected by the giver. There should be a fourth alternative of course, that of accepting the gift and doing nothing at all. Since the bribe is not protected by law or morality, this would seem to be the most logical behavior, and yet it is rarely done. One of the most astounding features of the bribe is the honesty of the receiver in delivering his return-service. Having accepted the bribe as a gift, he usually lives up to the law of the gift and faithfully does what is expected of him. The absence of the comforting psychological effect of the true gift does not prevent the receiver from acting as if it were present. In the case of a big bribe he may feel flattered because he is thought to be important enough to perform the service required. On the other hand, he may see the small routine bribe as a fee, a payment for a service implying no lasting personal ties. The dividing line between gift and bribe is not always clear. There is urgent need for further studies in this unreconnoitered field about which we hardly know anything for certain. Even such a reputable anthropologist as Tylor had difficulties with it. His theory of sacrifice is based on a definition of the concept that is much closer to the bribe than to the gift (Tylor 1871, II p. 375; Van Baal 1975).

Because a gift is addressed to the receiver's person, the giver usually cannot announce what he wishes to receive in return, a rule strictly respected in the Trobriand *kula*. Another and more important consequence is that the gift must take full account of the receiver's position and situation in relation to the giver. Situations are of two kinds, those concerning the receiver alone, and those defined by the relation between giver and receiver. The specific situation of the receiver need not occupy us for long. It is more or less a matter of course that a present given on the occasion of a death or sudden accident differs from that connected with the celebration of a feast. More important are the differences in status to which we shall return presently, and the group connections between the partners that must have our attention first.

If the receiver belongs to a different community, we may expect the deliverance of the gift to express social distance, probably by a more or less ceremonial form. If giver and receiver both belong to the same community, for example a joint family, there is little opportunity for explicit gift-exchange. Rather, the expression of partnership occurs in the continuous process of give-and-take that is characteristic of daily cooperation and that we described as generalized reciprocity. In their mutual relations, the We-notion prevails. It takes full account of individual differences, of age, sex, and bodily conditions. Everyone contributes to the common weal in accordance with his abilities. Inside the group, reciprocity is predominantly negatively defined. In a we-situation, questions of reciprocity do not easily arise, because there is no polarity, hence no counterpart relationship. The group prevails. But when one of the members of the group does not comply with reasonable expectations of co-operative behavior, he places himself in opposition to his group and will be questioned about the balance of his contributions to 'us', the solidary majority.

Finally, we must turn to differences as important disturbers of balance. In our own culture, where differences are as important as anywhere else, we have developed a special attitude vis-à-vis differences. Natural differences, such as those of age and sex, are readily accepted (but note that the latter is losing importance!). Social differences – and we tend to classify all other differences than those of sex and age as social or socially generated – are subject to suspicion. We look askance at those who are different, if we do not condemn them openly. A famous political dogma states that 'all men are created equal', a contention strongly rejected by modern ethologists (cf. Ardrey 1970 p. 36). Without subscribing to their approach, we might take to heart their appreciation of the significance of differences in nature. In each and every species, the individuals belonging to the species differ among themselves. The differences are not great; they all fall within the limits set by the morphological, physiological, and behavioral standard patterns of the species. Yet, they exist, and what is more, they are necessary. Without these individual differences there would be neither variation nor evolution. Taking a more sophisticated view, we might well ask whether our condemnation of social differences is not as much a prejudice as is their acceptance in cultures where they are recognized as an integral part of the world-order. They define a person's place in that order, and this is why he who *is* more, has to give more. We argued that 'giving is the offering of one's self as a partner'. The statement is incomplete; it should be amplified by adding: 'asking to be accepted as one actually is in society'. A chief cannot give a minor present without being mean, nor can a social nobody give a magnificent gift without being offensively ostentatious. The order of the gift must reflect the social positions of giver and receiver. In gift-exchange one cannot accept another personally without accepting him or her socially, along with what is inalienable to the other's place in society. This is why reciprocity cannot be more balanced than are the respective positions of persons. These positions define their places in their respective worlds, and membership in these worlds is the most fundamental requirement for a meaningful existence.

The balance of reciprocity can be upset by influences other than personal differences. One of these is power, the ability to take forcibly what cannot willingly be acquired. Another is indifference or an aversion to exert oneself to ensure one's rightful dues. We shall not discuss these deviations since they are not concerned with reciprocity proper. Unfortunately, we also have to abandon the discussion of a problem that certainly makes part of the subject matter: that is the compelling force exerted by the form of a transaction on subsequent behavior. We noted this force when we dealt with contract and bribe, but we evaded the question of what there is in the human mind that gives these forms such power over it. Why should a perverted gift-form, the bribe, so often be permitted to follow the law of the gift? This is a question that leads straight to the core of structuralism. It is impossible to answer this question here. Much subsidiary research of the 'grammar' of gift and bribe is needed before we can hope for a more precise answer to this problem than the one given above.

8 Reciprocity in the Administration of Justice

In modern law the principle of reciprocity is embodied in the general principle of equity, and in the elaborate differentiation of maximal punishments for trespasses and crimes according to their relative seriousness. This differentiation is deeply integrated in our culture. Every boy knows and expects that breaking a big windowpane calls for harsher punishment than that of a small one. Moreover, if he breaks the neighbor's windowpane he or his father will have to pay for it. There are two things involved here: the trespass and the indemnification for damages, and we usually keep them strictly apart as cases of criminal and civil law respectively.

In simple societies, legal authority is weak and a judiciary is almost or altogether absent. Our differentiation between criminal and civil law is lacking here, or present in an incipient form at best. If, in case of a sale, payment is deferred, the claimant can press the debtor. It may take him some time and much pressure, but ordinarily he will be paid. It is different when one of the parties in a sales transaction really cheats the other. The latter will become angry; he feels hurt, and his feelings of regret over the loss are intensified by those that result from the injury: he is hurt that he, personally, should be made the victim of this foul act. A wrong suffered, whether it be theft, insult, bodily injury or cheating, is experienced by the victim as an injury to his person. As a gift establishes or strengthens social relations, a wrong rends them. And as a gift arouses feelings of gratitude, a tort or a wrong stirs anger. Where the gift recognizes the receiver's position and status in his universe, a wrong impairs them, throwing the victim out of his place in, and out of his state of relative harmony with his universe. The gift evokes a countergift that affirms the proper status of donor and donee, and cements the personal relations between them; a wrong calls for revenge, which reaffirms the status of the injured party and humiliates the malefactor.

The reciprocity of revenge has emotional overtones that, if not stronger, are significantly more obvious than those associated with gift-exchange. In other respects, we find a curious parallelism. An insult inflicted by a person of low status on one of high status is avenged more severely than if the victim were an equal. It is a greater insult, just as the small gift given by the poor to the rich is judged to be more valuable because it derives from one who has little to give. There is also a parallelism in reverse. A delay in making a return-gift may result in the offer of a return-gift of higher value than the initial one. Revenge, if delayed, tends to become more moderate. Putting it somewhat differently: in gift-exchange, if the countergift follows the gift immediately, perfect balance is the rule. On the other hand, if revenge is inflicted on the spot, it tends to be well in excess of the gravity of the insult, whereas it will be better balanced if the injured party has had time 'to cool down'.

The effect of the time-lag is well exemplified by what happens to the Australian aboriginal who elopes with another man's wife (cf. Berndt 1965 pp. 293 ff.; Meggitt 1962 p. 101; Spencer & Gillen 1927 II, pp. 467 ff.). The offenders are pursued and, if overtaken, probably killed. If they manage to escape, a year or so may be allowed to elapse before negotiations are opened concerning the possibility of their return. If return is agreed upon, the offenders have to submit to an ordeal. The male offender has to meet the plaintiff in a public meeting. He stands unarmed, listening to the abuse that the wronged husband heaps upon him before he starts throwing spears at the adulterer. The latter is allowed a shield to fend off the missiles, but in the end he must be hit anyhow, because blood must be drawn. A wound in a thigh suffices, but if he has bad luck, he may even be killed. In the meantime, her kinsmen (in some cases her former husband) take the woman and give her a sound thrashing, hard enough to leave her beaten up and bruised for some time to come. After the ordeal, the two are reaccepted by the group and may settle as husband and wife. The process reflects the effects of reciprocity. At the discovery of his wife's elopement the wronged husband feels deeply offended and will kill the adulterers if he can. It is his right. After a year his initial hurt and anger have calmed down. He may have considered that the runaway wife was, after all, not a good partner, or have found comfort with another wife. Still, the affront must be avenged. But by now it can be avenged in a manner more in keeping with the measure of the wronged party's less urgent grief.

We err if we content ourselves with the notion of a balance of feelings. Feelings are not easily measurable and are fickle besides. It is more important to determine what has been accomplished by the ordeal. A conflict has been settled and normal relations have been restored. The ordeal has publicly affirmed the wrong of the offenders and the right of the plaintiff. The former have paid for their offence by means of the harm inflicted upon them, the latter is restored to his personal status in the group (not as husband of that particular woman!) by carrying out the role of executioner granted to him and, in general, by the public recognition of his rights. It goes a bit far to say that the loss of the wife has been balanced by the harm suffered by the offenders. The balance is a muddled one, as muddled as it is in any form of generalized reciprocity. Yet the ordeal has the same effect as an exchange of gifts. A reconciliation is achieved, and the proper means to that end is the act of atonement that restores the penitent to his position in the group.

Atonement and consecutive restoration of the culprit to his rightful place in the group are the fundamental aim of every punishment. Punishment differs from revenge, which severs the social ties that punishment is eager to restore. The social intentions of punishment betray the group's interest; it is not without reason that so often punishment must be inflicted under the supervision of the authority concerned – in Australia the local group, in other areas a chief or a village head. A telling example of effective punishment among the Cheyenne is reported by Hoebel (1954 pp. 151 f.). Two young men, disregarding the chief's orders to stay in camp in abeyance of a common attack on an approaching herd of buffaloes, set out to chase the herd on their own account. They were soon discovered and overtaken: their horses killed, their guns broken, and they themselves slashed with a riding whip. They then got a severe admonition by the chief to which they listened in silence. Now the chief relented and, after some deliberation, they were given new horses and guns. Restored to their positions and rights, they returned to the group as members under an obligation. This was a form of punishment that, after a serious misdemeanor, a son might have received from his father. In the family, too, atonement reintroduces the sinner into the family circle as a member with an obligation.

Revenge, on the other hand, is an act of hostility, leading not to the restoration of social ties, but to their complete severance. It is for this reason that capital punishment can hardly be called a punishment. In fact, it does not even have the form of a punishment. A punishment begins with the execution of the penalty, capital punishment ends with it. This does not mean that capital punishment is necessarily unjust;

the culprit's misdemeanor may have been so serious as to exclude him from his group, making readmission impossible. He has acted as an enemy, and he is treated as such. Capital punishment is an act of war, a revenge. The reciprocity of the reaction can be perfect, even sublime. It is reciprocity of the same order as that applied in the exchange called trade, cold and calculated. The offender is no longer a person or fellow member, but an enemy.

Revenge is the natural reaction of the individual to a tort. The tort has a humiliating effect because it is a negation of the victim's position in society. His reaction is necessarily violent. It is not simply the material loss or the nuisance but, above all, the attack on his person that counts. Revenge is by nature unbalanced; the victim must show himself superior to the offender by hitting back harder than he has been hit himself. The position of being victimized must be reversed into that of victor. Superiority is demonstrated by giving more in return than was received, whether it be blows, insults, or valuables. It is the same principle of recognition of personal status, but here it works in reverse. It is not the personal status of the receiver that is at stake but that of the giver. He yearns for its reparation and achieves it by delivering a superior gift of blows.

Private revenge has a ruinous effect on community life, and weakly organized societies often suffer considerably from the consequences of a wrong committed by one of their members. It is urgent that reparation be made and, lacking effective machinery for the enforcement of law, societies follow various ways to restore peace. Our present interest is not in these endeavors, but in the interpretation given to the rule of reciprocity. We have been taught to believe that among the less civilized it is 'an eye for an eye, a tooth for a tooth'. It hardly ever is. In the case of homicide, the application of the rule can only result in the progressive weakening of the group. The solution is found in the payment of *weregild*, a substantial gift that pretends to be an adequate equivalent for a life. The two elements are too dissimilar ever to justify an equation. Primitive societies are not inferior to modern civilization in this respect. The same dissimilarity prevails in our legal practice that remands a homicide to prison for a number of years. Where not goods but persons are concerned, reciprocity cannot be rigorously balanced, and the principle is amended accordingly. Again, the group prevails, as it does in a we-situation.

The realm where balanced reciprocity is most at home is civil law. The amount of an indemnity is carefully calculated to be the exact equivalent of the loss inflicted. Unimpeded by emotions or violent feelings, the legal process goes its way to the realization of balance and equity. The situation changes when persons are involved. All sorts of secondary considerations and emotions enter the judicial ring with them, and not only among the less civilized. In 1932 the French President Doumer was murdered by a man who, to all intents and purposes, was a psychopath. If he had killed the grocer around the corner, he would have been sent to a lunatic asylum. But he killed a president, an act of war, and he went straight to the guillotine. Reason and unreason, arithmetic and passion alternately affect the application of the rule of reciprocity, deciding for balance or imbalance, for reconciliation or war, for friendship or competition. Yet the rule stands, guiding the individual along his path to full membership and participation in his universe, a membership proper to him alone, a participation ultimately deciding on the modes of application of the golden rule.

9 *Conclusion*

Reciprocity presupposes interaction between two elements (parties) who communicate by means of an exchange in which each maintains its identity. If the elements make part of a we-group, interaction and exchange are frequent, but the elements themselves remain relatively in the background, the identity of the interactors being veiled by the embracing we-relation. Reciprocity is latent, informal, and generalized; questions of formal reciprocity arise only in case of failure, as when a derelict member of the group maneuvers himself into the position of disputed membership.

If the identity of each of the elements is clear and if they are considered functionally as each other's equals, the ensuing exchange will be one of balanced recprocity. If the elements are seen as functionally unequal, the balance of reciprocity is affected accordingly.

Every exchange is an act of communication, but there are two types of communication that must be clearly discerned. In the first, communication is identical with the exchange itself; in the second communication involves the inclusion of the exchange-partners in an embracing whole. The first type is strongly favored by communication theory; the goods, services, and messages that are exchanged, are considered as objects in a context of unrestricted interchangeability in which the exchange value is the sole criterion. Perfect balance, expressing the functional equality of the elements (the parties exchanging) prevails, but there is no guarantee that each of the parties shall live up to the obligations of the rule. A guarantee must be derived from an institution possessed of power and created for the protection of contractual obligations and rights. The development of trade and the increase of contractual transactions go hand in hand with the growth of the state and its legal machinery.

In the second type of communication, the objects exchanged function as vehicles of intentions that are expressive of common bonds. They are gifts. Here the elements (the transactors) are not merely seen in their functions of giver and receiver, but in their proper place and situation in the society as a whole, a place that is confirmed and strengthened by the transaction. Since its basic ingredient is the friendly intention of the giver, gift-exchange must be free from the intervention of authorities; it is a social act that derives its value from individual intentions, and thus contributes to the increase of social solidarity. Moreover, the giver is not in any need of legal protection because his gift, which confirms the receiver in his social position, carries with it his automatic rejection if the receiver fails to reciprocate.

The gift owes its compelling force to its confirmation of the partners' participation in a meaningful whole. The exchange affirms that giver and receiver are integral parts of their universe. The gift retains this power of affirmation even in its perverted forms as weapons in competition and as bribes. The competitive form has been well studied, and its binding force is adequately explained in terms of its notoriously public character. Further studies of the bribe, which lacks this public character, are urgently needed. Without in the least suggesting a precedence of form over content, we strongly hold that a study of the meaning of form in the bribe would contribute substantially to a better understanding of the ways and means of interpersonal communication, especially if combined with the study of other deviant forms that, for the sake of brevity, had to be left unexplored in the present essay[9].

We have argued that the rule of reciprocity operates in exchange transactions according to the dictates of social position. This has been confirmed by our analysis of the administration of justice. In civil lawsuits concerned with the exchange value of interchangeable goods and services, the rule of balanced reciprocity is paramount. Criminal lawsuits, however, affect the place of plaintiff and defendant in society. Again, reciprocity is adapted to the exigencies of social reality. The rigor of the rule is mitigated by replacing revenge with punishment, thus aiming at the restoration of the social order through atonement and subsequent reconciliation.

The analysis leads to the surprising conclusion that reciprocity is best balanced and least impeded by conflicting pressures where social ties are weak; it can be anything from balanced to unbalanced or muddled where social solidarity is strong and social differences are recognized. This result calls for a 'conclusion de morale' after the style of Mauss.

Modern civilization is allergic to social differences. Ever since the publication in 1755 of the *Discourse on the Origin and Basis of Inequality among Men* by Jean-Jacques Rousseau, our civilization has emphasized the value of social equality as the guarantor of

[9] The fee and the bride-price (the 'marriage gift' agreed upon after prolonged bargaining) are intriguing cases.

freedoms, such as the freedom of thought, the freedom of expression of opinion, the freedom to produce, in short, the freedom to be oneself and to do everything to promote self-realization without impinging on the self-realization of others. What do men do who wish to reform their society in a way that guarantees optimal equality and personal freedom? They choose themselves a model conducive to that end. Rejecting the institutions connected with the model of the gift, such as patronage, personal bondage, social welfare by charity, and hereditary relations between squire and tenants, eighteenth-century man chose easily. He decided upon trade as his model, with all parties equal, personally uncommitted by their transactions, with everything perfectly balanced and permitting a fair degree of anonymity. It is not by chance that Karl Marx followed Adam Smith in his presentation of labor as a commodity that is for sale, a ware that must be made the object of hard bargaining. The implementation of the model has been a success; wages have been raised considerably, the old forms of patronage have been abolished without exception, there is formal equality for everyone, and where its realization falls short of expectations, every political party makes promises to remedy the gap.

Such promises are empty for two reasons. The first is that our preference for the model of trade is correlative to our material wealth. Archaic societies must adhere to the model of the gift for the simple reason that here wealth is limited to a very restricted variety of goods which, when available in considerable quantities, can only be utilized by giving them away. Modern wealth, however, can be converted into a virtually unlimited variety of goods that all concur to make life more agreeable. The second reason is that our society combines the ideal of equality with a partly conscious, partly subconscious preference for inequality. In an analysis of the role of competition in games and education published elsewhere (Van Baal 1974) I have demonstrated at some length that our preferences for achievement have successfully turned the rules of equal opportunity and equal rules for everyone into effective instruments for the realization and permanence of inequality.

Young people today complain that social relations suffer from a lack of warmth. Of course they do; they are as cold as the stock exchange. We chose the model of trade, and relations will become colder still because everyone expects the remedy from more equality, more freedom, and greater anonymity. Social warmth can only thrive where the Other is recognized and accepted in his otherness, that is, where he is known as a person. But this can only happen where relatively small, local groups still have a function. Social warmth is not possible in a society in which the individual is but an anonymous case.

However, this is not the place to enlarge on the troubles of modern society, or on the contrarieties of our culture, which combines the ideal of integral equality with strong preferences for competition and achievement. In this context we must content ourselves with the simple conclusion that reciprocity is a universal rule for all human relations, but has its more beneficent and, above all, its more humanizing effects where the application of the rule is mitigated by considerations of respect and compassion for the Other's person because he is one of us, part of a community.

II

The part of women in the marriage trade: objects or behaving as objects?[1]

In his book *Les Structures élémentaires de la Parenté* Cl. Lévi-Strauss has cogently argued that in the different forms of marriage trade prevailing in a large majority of traditional societies it is the women who circulate between groups of men. Setting apart the small number of societies practising matrilocal marriage where conditions are different[2], and leaving the case of modern marriage institutions out of discussion altogether, any student of Asian, African or Australian societies has to admit that women do circulate between groups of men. The evidence is overwhelming and, up to an extent, we cannot but agree with Lévi-Strauss when he states, 'Traiter la filiation patrilinéaire et la filiation matrilinéaire, la résidence patrilocale et la résidence matrilocale, comme des éléments abstraits qu'on combine deux à deux au nom du simple jeu des

---

[1] The present article is the English version of an address delivered at the conference organized at the University of Utrecht in september 1970 to honour Professor H. Th. Fischer on the occasion of his retirement.

[2] Umar Junus (1964 pp. 303, 312, 318) presents evidence that in the matrilocal and matrilineal society of the Minangkabau it is sometimes the groom and not the bride who is given away.

probabilités, c'est donc méconnaître totalement la situation initiale, qui inclut les femmes au nombre des objets sur lesquels portent les transactions entre les hommes' (Lévi-Strauss 1949 p. 136). I have no difficulty in subscribing to the hypothesis that patrilocal residence is more fundamental and takes precedence over matrilocal institutions. Neither do I deny that women are included among the objects transferred by and between men. Yet, I must raise a question here. Are women simply objects, as has repeatedly been stated by Lévi-Strauss (cf. inter alia op. cit. pp. 38, 43, 73-76, 135) or do they agree to be objects, i.e. subjects willingly agreeing to behave as objects?

The difference is important but, unfortunately, Lévi-Strauss did not pay attention to it, at least not in this context. It is not that he really thinks of women as just objects. Later on in his book, *Les Structures élémentaires*, as also in his *Anthropologie Structurale* (pp. 326 ff.), he emphasizes that women must be seen as persons. In his theory of marriage, however, he presents them as values, and as values only. The object-role of the women in the marriage trade monopolizes the argument to the extent of ignoring the possibility that this role, instead of being a matter of passive submission to the orders of the males, could be the outcome of some form of female preference. The male bias is evident. We need not blame him for this, as other famous theories (those of Freud, for instance) are not a whit better in this respect. The male point of view dominates in various social theories. Although a theory which does not pay much attention to the female point of view is not necessarily wrong, its bias certainly gives ample reason for critical reflection. In the case of Lévi-Strauss's theory of marriage the fact that women are treated as objects necessarily raises

71

the question why the women do agree to be objects, or, if the question is assumed to be unanswerable, whether it is feasible for women to be turned into objects without their agreeing to it.

It is not a simple question of yes or no. We have to admit that the low social position of women in many traditional societies is highly suggestive of the assumption that they simply are at the mercy of the men who know how to bully them into submissiveness. A well-documented case of contemptuous and oppressive treatment of women is that of the secret rituals celebrated in Australia and New Guinea. Every time the men wish to celebrate a religious ceremony the women are chased away by the frightening sound of the bull-roarers. Nevertheless, everywhere we find proof that all the time the men depend on the active co-operation of these very same women and, what is more, that they are well aware of this. Structurally the women cannot be dispensed with in the ritual. The importance of the ritual is based on secret knowledge and there is no secret unless there be a category of uninitiated. The terror of the gods, symbolized by the shrieking of the bullroarers and supported by frightening stories told to the uninitiated (primarily the women), requires the terrorized. The impressive show staged by the men needs an admiring public. The magnificent masks exhibited at the end of the Orokolo *hevehe*-ritual would lose all their value if the admiring women were not there to meet the performers when, at last, they descend from the men's house (Williams, 1940, ch. 22-24). The fright of the women, combined with their absence from the execution of the secret episodes of the ritual and their respectful, admiring presence on the occasion of its public stages, are structural prerequisites to the secret ceremony. What is true structurally is also true psychologically. By letting themselves be frightened and running away, but yet remaining near enough to witness those aspects of the ceremony which they should behold, the women contribute substantially to the psychological effect of the ritual, confirming the men in their belief that what they are doing is something very important. It is hard to imagine what would happen if the women, instead of being terrified, called out 'boo' at the moment when the sound of the bullroarer warns them that now it is time to be afraid, or if the women should refuse to prepare the festive meal or to co-operate at the right moment in the sexual disorder which is part of the celebration. Fortunately, the women do co-operate. They always do, but why? Is it because they are frightened, expecting to be beaten if they do not comply?

The fact that their fright makes part of the show which depends both structurally and psychologically on exactly these negative forms of co-operation belies the assumption that fear of the men is the main motive for the women in their faithful role-fulfilment. Their negative collaboration is a case of active co-operation, not of mere submission. The men depend on it and if the women refuse, the men are nowhere, and by no means in the case of ritual only. Female co-operation is most obviously needed in the case of marriage. A woman who runs away from her husband jeopardizes the relations between two groups, perhaps even between three. If an angry woman refuses to collect food, her husband goes hungry, and it would be an easy thing for women collectively to withdraw their cooperation if in their highhandedness the men should overstep the mark.

The case of the women is not really such a weak one

as is often surmised, certainly not under more primitive conditions, such as those prevailing in Australia (Berndt, 1964 pp. 94, 104 ff.; Meggit, 1957 p. 143). They collect all the vegetable food as well as the mites of animal food such as insects, shells and so on. If we make up the balance of the contributions made by each of the two sexes to the daily board in Australia, the men are decidedly the losers. The activities of the two sexes and their share in the provisions for the life and welfare of the community have been tabulated below. The enumeration clearly shows that the women excel in economic activities, the men in ritual ones. The table mirrors the division of labour between the sexes, but we can also conceive of it as a survey of a system of perpetual exchange of goods and services between the sexes. In this particular context the economic contribution made by the males, confined to the provision with game, is of specific interest. The game caught by the males is not simply a contribution to the common board of their own household; a choice part of the meat goes to the wife's relatives. In other words, the division of labour between the sexes is indeed at the same time a system of exchange between the two sexes, the economic contribution by the males functioning also as a payment for the services rendered by the vegetable-food-providing females, a payment presented to the fathers and brothers who kindly relinquished them to their present husbands.

The Australian case should not be unduly generalized, though there are a good many tribes outside Australia among whom the female contribution to the economy does not fall far below the Australian standards. The really important fact is that it is exactly in Australia, where women are excluded from ritual and their role

MALES	FEMALES
animal food (30% of the calories)	vegetable and lesser animal food (70% of the calories)
protection, warfare, fighting	procreation of children, preparation of daily food, care of all members of the family
ritual performance	minor services to ritual performers; mourning and bewailing the dead
sex	sex

TABLE 1.

Provision of goods and services by each of the sexes

as objects in the marriage trade is uncommonly evident, that the economic contribution of the females is such a substantial one that it is impossible to ignore their services as the main providers of food and care. It is obvious that men who exchange women between them, exchange the most valuable goods imaginable. Women are more productive than men, in other words, economically men are more in need of women than women are of men. For men to do without women is more difficult than it is for women to do without men. Therefore it is also natural that men are more persistently in search of women than women are of men. Under such conditions it is more probable that men will exchange women between them than that women exchange men. When all is said and done, women – also procreators of children – are more valuable than men. Apart from all this, it is questionable whether a system of groups of women exchanging men between them could work at all. The main pragmatic contribution of the males being game and protection, a system of close inter-male cooperation is a primary condition for a successful fulfilment of these tasks. Certainly in warfare the men should be able to act in solidarity, an extremely difficult if not impossible charge for a group of mutually unrelated men originating from a variety of competing groups who must derive their common bond from the fortuitous circumstance that they have been picked by women belonging to one group.

There are other arguments to explain why women do not exchange men, but those presented here suffice to demonstrate that women are the most precious goods which can possibly be exchanged between groups and that – if persons have to be exchanged between groups – it must necessarily be women and not men who, in the process of the exchange, lose the better part of their ability to fulfil their proper roles. All this, however, does not imply or explain that women must be exchanged as objects, almost as objects among other valuables. There is no real evidence confirming that they are. On the contrary, all the evidence we have tends to confirm that they are exchanged because they agree to be exchanged. Actually, it is their great asset and merit that they do. By agreeing to be exchanged a sister enables her brother himself to marry. By agreeing to be married off she renders her brother an important and lasting service, lasting at least as long as her marriage endures. In terms of the gift, this implies that by her consent to be married off the sister creates a claim on her brother for the full duration of her marriage. It is a claim for the brother's protection to be given to her and to her future children.

By consenting to being married off, the sister, physically the weaker, secures for herself a strong position. Her claim on her brother's protection for herself and her future children implies that her brother must have the right as well as the duty to intervene in the affairs of the family she is going to establish as a result of her marriage. It is exactly the kind of claim her position allows her to make. She avails herself of the weak position of her brother, who is her debtor, vis-à-vis herself, as well as of the weak position of her husband vis-à-vis her brother (or initially, her father who in due time will be substituted as head of the woman's family of origin by her brother). Her husband, being as the bride-taker the debtor of his wife's brother, is not in a position that he can refuse the latter's intervention (or, as it is put euphemistically in family circles: his cooperation) in family matters. The husband has to accept his wife's brother's authority. By the simple act of agreeing to be given away in marriage to a man of another group the woman, wife to the one and sister to the other, has manoeuvred herself into an intermediary position allowing her to manipulate. Two men protect her. The one owes a debt to the other and the other owes one to her (cf. fig. 1). Her strength is that her position allows her to manipulate. It is exactly what she needs because, apart from physically being the weaker, she is also going to be a mother.

The woman's prospective motherhood is a point of fundamental importance, so fundamental as to make

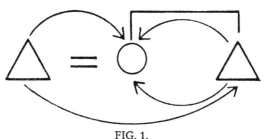

FIG. 1.
upper arrows: protection
lower arrows: indebtedness

it seem commonplace to make mention of it. However, it is not commonplace at all, it is a fact which because of its plain evidence is altogether too often taken for granted and consequently ignored and forgotten. Motherhood is not a woman's accidental fate, it is the very essence of her existence. Margaret Mead cogently pointed out that in traditional society every woman knows that she is going to be a mother (Mead, 1949 pp. 81 ff.). Women are mothers or preparing themselves to be mothers, and motherhood conditions their behaviour and gives shape to their ways of life and their outlook. It is only the blessed myopy caused by their vanity which prevents men from perceiving that women are always mothers, also in their relations with men. The women cannot help it, neither can the men be blamed for failing to note this. The terrified women running away when the bullroarers sound, the proud women holding torches aloft to make their beautifully adorned males show off in their glory during the nocturnal dance, the indulgent women participating in sexual promiscuity, the ambitious women encouraging their husbands to stand for parliament, they are all mothers, each in turn patting her husband's (or – as the case may be – her lover's) shoulder, ensuring him that he did excellently when all went well, giving him the comfort that it was not his fault when it all turned out wrong. It is a mother's job to encourage, as everybody knows who ever took time to observe a mother with a toddler making his first steps.

My eulogy of women should not be misunderstood. There is nothing sentimental in it; actually I am only trying to define the role of women in human society. The recognition that, basically, motherhood is its core leads us back from considerations mainly of a psychological nature straightaway to the structural argument. Motherhood is the basis of all kinship and in a structural analysis of kinship women necessarily must be seen in the perspective of motherhood, because it is this which lays the foundation for the permanence of the intergroup relations commonly referred to as kinship. A father is expendable, but there is no kinship without motherhood. Therefore, a further reconnaissance of the mother-role is in order. Mothers provide for succour, food, care, comfort and emotional security. The mother-role implies a liberal measure of other-directedness, an other-directedness primarily focused on her own children, but easily extended to other persons: a husband, a lover, a brother. We can dismiss the question whether some such thing as a mother-instinct does exist. The process of a girl's growing up, her education and early conditioning concur to prepare her for a mother-role. It is enough for us to know that here we are moving in the uncertain borderland where nature and culture merge. The two points of real interest to us are, first, the tremendous importance of women not only as bearers of children but also as providers of motherly care and succour. They are, indeed, the most valuable goods a group can bestow on the members of another group. In the second place, the focal position of motherhood in a woman's life explains why women, when agreeing to co-operate in the marriage trade, identify themselves with their offspring and, claiming protection for themselves by their brothers, make this claim for their children as well. For a girl marriage means motherhood. The two are inseparable. As a married woman she is going to be a mother and the contemplation of marriage is necessarily the contemplation of future motherhood. The brother who is indebted to his sister for her willingness to be married off, is naturally indebted to her children as well, because these children are, to the sister, part of herself. Actually, these children are the raison d'être of the whole transaction.

The argument expounded here finds strong support in the pivotal position allowed to the brother-sister relationship in a wide variety of kinship systems, and in the strong emphasis given to the mother's brother – sister's child relationship in an equally large, or perhaps even more widely spread number of divergent societies. The brother is the protector of his sister; in societies stressing the value of premarital chastity he even becomes the guardian of her honour. There is hardly a more astonishing and contradictory mystification than this romantic quality in a woman, her honour. Her honour is the glory of the family and its loss is felt as the most serious misfortune which can befall the group. In spite of the lofty phraseology glorifying the girl's honour, its material locus is a minute and contemptible part of the body which has no other function than to perturb poor girls when it is not as unimpaired as convention prescribes. If something is said or done to the detriment of their sister's honour, brothers in various societies react with an over-sensitiveness bordering on madness or even worse. It is not only the medieval nobleman who goes berserk at an injurious remark concerning his sister's behaviour. The Murngin brother – little interested in chastity generally – feeling that his sister's honour is affected by a casual outburst of erotic abuse, reacts like a madman (Lloyd Warner, 1958 pp. 66, 110 ff.[3]);

3 The subject was re-investigated and discussed by Hiatt in 1964. His comment led to a renewed discussion between Makarius and Hiatt (1966), and recently to a structural interpretation by K. Maddock (1970).

and the Macassarese girl who realizes that she has lost her honour has to flee to save her life (Chabot, 1950 p. 213). Examples could be cited from many parts of the world; the point is that the girl being the best, the most valuable, the most enduring present any family can make to another, is necessarily her family's most exquisite property, its pride and glory. In societies observing strict norms of sexual behaviour, the girl's glory easily becomes associated with her virginity which should be kept untainted until the moment that she is handed over to the bridegroom whose first task is to accomplish defloration.

A brother is necessarily deeply interested in his sister's behaviour before her marriage, particularly so in cultures where a young woman's virginity is highly valued. Once she is married the brother not only continues to be interested in his sister's behaviour, he usually is even more interested than ever before. This is well borne out by the surprising fact that in so many societies men who, as co-respondents, should know better, proclaim in all honesty that it is the women who are the cause of adultery and of all the interfamily tensions and troubles ensuing from it. The accusation betrays the worry of the brothers over the possibility that their sisters might not live up to their part of the bargain by adhering faithfully to their legal spouses. The brothers, from their own escapades with other men's sisters, know fully well how easily sisters may fail them. They do not wish their own sister to do the same, as any disturbance of her marriage might upset their own relations with her husband's group and eventually even affect their own marriage relations. The brothers feel very strongly that their sisters should not fail in the fulfilment of their part of the deal. On the contrary, the sisters should forestall the troubles caused by their brothers' own philanderous habits and any failure of a woman in this respect is an act of bad faith which cannot possibly be laid to the charge of the men because the men have a real interest in keeping things straight. The men are contractually committed among each other, they are indebted to their own marriage relations. Women are not indebted (cf. below, fig. 2) and therefore irresponsible and dangerous.

The position of a brother vis-à-vis his sister is plainly ambiguous. If a runaway wife takes refuge with her brother, he will not hesitate to bring her back to her husband. He does not wish her marriage to break down because his own interests are at stake. Nevertheless, the greatest caution should be exercised. He should not be too unfair to her lest she become desperate which might result in her running away with another man. In that case the last would be far worse than the first because not only a brawl, but a serious fight might become inevitable. The sister should remain under a moral obligation to her family of origin, primarily to her brother. She should realize that it is up to her to be a good sister as well as a faithful wife. To that end it is essential that the brother observe his obligations to her and her children. He must remonstrate with her husband if the latter should have treated her badly, and he must act the good and obliging uncle to her children. A sister who feels that she is forsaken by her brother and neglected by her family of origin, is dangerous. She is capable of any mischief. Actually, it is her brother who is indebted to her, and not she to him, and if this brother fails her she may react irresponsibly.

The ambiguity of the brother's position more or less equals that of the sister, which is ambiguous by definition. The price paid for the advantages of exogamous marriage is high and one wonders why people do not more often try to compromise between the exigencies of exogamy and the advantages of upholding the perpetuation of the undivided family by resorting to matrilocal marriage. The answer is that the compromise is neither fish nor fowl. We have already noted that a reversal of the rule that women are exchanged between groups of males does not occur. There is no clear case of an exchange of males between groups of women. In the few cases where an exchange of males is reported, it is the leading males who are the organizers of the exchange. Apparently there is something in the nature of males which precludes the realization of an exchange of males between groups of females. It is always the males who exercise authority, and this applies also in matrilineal societies practising uxorilocal marriage[4]. In such societies the husband's position is uncertain even for the leading males who are either the visiting husbands of women of another group, or the residents in their own group (that of their mothers and sisters) living in virilocal marriage. A situation of this kind is unsatisfactory to all concerned. In the first place, there is no real exchange of women between groups except in as far as the leading males are concerned who managed to marry virilocally. The visiting husband does not become a member of his wife's group. When husbands settle with their wives' groups they remain strangers,

[4] In this context M. Kay Martin's study of matrilineal and matrilocal South American Foragers (Martin 1969) is of interest. Unfortunately details concerning the residence rules after marriage in connection with the authority pattern within the matrilineal and matrilocal group are lacking. An additional study of these aspects is needed.

each subject to the authority of his wife's brothers who are the real leaders of the group. The loyalties of these in-marrying husbands either remain divided between their own and their wife's group, or they have to accept a dependent position which denies them proper rights in the group which they have adopted. In any case the position is unsatisfactory and, what is most important of all, this form of marriage does not result in strong ties between the groups of bride-givers and bride-takers. The bride is not really given away, she is retained; she remains under the authority of her brother, c.q. her mother's brother. The sister's position in matrilocal marriage differs widely from the one she acquires through virilocal marriage. Virilocal marriage turns mother's brother and brother into protectors who are indebted to the woman because she willingly agreed to behave as an object in the marriage trade. By marrying matrilocally she does not oblige her brother. The brother's gains are small because he loses little and does not give her away. His actual role is that of an authority, and the same holds true of the mother's brother. They are not indebted to their sisters or sisters' children. As a matter of fact, they own them. The children the woman bears her husband are not her husband's but her brother's heirs, and the father's position with regard to his children tends to become restricted to little more than that of a friend who cannot really assert his influence with their mother's brother, who has the ultimate authority over his sister's children. The woman herself, remaining under the authority of her brother, is more dependent than she would be when, taking the risk of marrying out, she obliges her brother as well as her husband. She does not gain by matrilocal marriage because she does not take a risk. Worst of all, the compromise offered by matrilocal marriage is not a compromise at all. It does not succeed in removing the ambiguity from the brother-sister relation. Another and equally serious ambiguity slips in: the brother to whom the sister is sexually taboo becomes deeply involved in his sister's sexual life because she must bear him his heirs and successors. Here lies a source of new, disruptive tensions. In this context Burridge's description of the brother-sister relationship among the Tangu is instructive (Burridge, 1969 pp. 105 ff.).

In conclusion we state that the women, too, have good reasons to prefer marrying out. It gives them an opportunity to state their terms. The expression should not be misinterpreted. It is not so that a woman, before she agrees to be married out, specifies her preferences and conditions. Normally, nothing of the kind happens. However, there is a code of rules and mores to which any woman can make an appeal. This code of rules and mores is not the simple product of male discretion but the outcome of an incessant tug-of-war between the sexes inside the family as well as inside the society at large. The supposition that a society's rules of conduct are exclusively or predominantly male-made is preposterous. The fact that the codification of the rules and the supervision of their observance very often are male prerogatives should not lead us to make the mistake of the cock perched on the hedge crowing because the hen laid an egg.

Now we are in a better position to consider the consequences of our rapid and necessarily rather sketchy analysis. It can be schematized in the simple diagram of fig. 2 in which the arrows stand for indebtedness, a double arrow indicating a high degree of indebtedness. It is interesting to note that the woman – wife to the one and sister to the other – has no debts. She

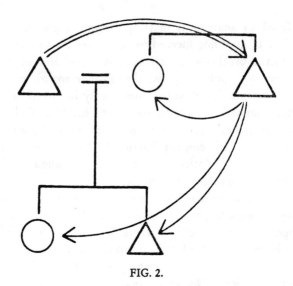

FIG. 2.

may be burdened with duties – as she undoubtedly is – but she has no debts. Here lies the strength of her position and the ground of the accusation that she is irresponsible.

The first and obvious inference to be made from the diagram is that any form of virilocal marriage, whether it be patrilocal or avunculocal, involves the recognition of the matriline, and not accidentally, as a secondary by-product of the marriage transaction, but as a structural condition of virilocal marriage as such. The relation between mother's brother and sister's son is not a matter of matrifiliation – a weak argument anyhow as Schneider has shown (1965) – but a relation ineluctably included in this type of marriage. The recognition of the matriline – whether implicit or explicit – is the reification of the brother's debt to his sister. The late J. P. B. de Josselin de Jong, when arguing that the bilineate is consistent with matrilateral cross-cousin marriage (1952 pp. 32 ff., 55 ff.), was even more right than he could then have realized; the bilineate is – structurally – at the root of every form of virilocal marriage. This does not mean that the bilineate will often be institutionalized; it can be present without being emphasized. Actually, institutionalized bilineality is necessarily rare. It means that the emphasis on either line is equally strong whereas the exigencies of social life normally favour the preferential application of one of the two. A good illustration can be borrowed from strictly patrilineal societies such as those of South New Guinea, the Marind-anim, the Keraki, the Kiwai, the Torres Straits Islanders. In spite of their explicit patrilineality, the relations between a mother's brother and a sister's child are very close and important. What else does such a close and affectionate tie mean but a recognition of the fact that any child, apart from being a member of its own family and patriclan, is at the same time a kind of non-resident member of its mother's group? The same happens to be the case in many African societies in which such customs occur as levirate and ghost-marriage, which can be interpreted as indications that a married woman is more or less the property of her husband's group. The strong position of the mother's brother in these societies gives evidence that in spite of all this the woman's membership of her family of origin is neither ignored nor effaced. On the contrary, it is a functionally important and effective reality in every family's life. All the evidence goes to confirm the correctness of our analysis which ultimately leads to the surprising conclusion that matrilineate is not the effect of matrilocal but of virilocal marriage.

A second important consequence of recognizing the women's willingness to behave as objects in the marriage trade as a constitutive factor in the structure of kinship, is the elucidation of the problems arising from the widely spread custom of (female) hypergamy. In its most simple form the problem is as follows. A marriage is based on the gift of a woman made by a group (the bride-givers) to a member of another group (the bride-takers). It is a gift of the highest value which can only be reciprocated by the countergift of another woman. If such a countergift is not effected, the bride-takers remain the debtors of the bride-givers even when and where they make an effort to redress the balance by the presentation of valuable goods to the bride-givers. In other words, bride-givers are superior (or senior, if a more moderate term be preferred) to bride-takers. The status of the bridegroom is lower than that of his bride's family and thus, by her marriage, the bride becomes a member of a lower status group. This, of course, does not imply that the groom's group is necessarily in every respect of lower status than its bride-giving group. The status implied is only that of affinal relationship and need not affect other status positions. Nevertheless, we might expect a generalizing effect of so recurrent a situation as that created by bride-taking without concomitant bride-giving. The expectation is not fulfilled; on the contrary, in many societies there is a definite trend towards the reverse; though women cannot be given in marriage to grooms of lower social rank, they may be married out to men of higher rank. The trend favouring hypergamy plainly conflicts with the fundamental rule, deriving from the structure of the gift, that the giver is superior to the recipient.

In Lévi-Strauss's discussion of the implications of hypergamy the problem is largely ignored because in his view compensation for the loss of a woman is possible by means of a payment in goods. Leach (1951) takes a similar stand, but he differs from Lévi-Strauss in that he strongly emphasizes the possibility that women by marrying do indeed take a step down the social ladder, and he illustrates his point with data derived from the Katchin, the Batak and the Lovedu. The Katchin and the Batak are of specific interest because in both cases there prevails a system of generalized exchange based on preferential marriage with a matrilateral cross-cousin. Among the Katchin, as also among the Batak, the superiority of the bride-givers to the bride-takers is evident and made explicit. Does this mean that by her marriage a bride loses in social status? According to Leach it does, at least in principle. He points out that marriages of women with men one class below them do occur and that this serves the useful function of strengthening the relations between the superior and the inferior groups by enlarging the latter's dependency on the former by means of affinal ties. Yet, Leach's argument is not wholly convincing. Though he denies that hypergamy occurs, he explains in a footnote (1951 p. 43, note 39) that chiefs and headmen may take women from a lower class. Also, the husbands of women marrying into a lower class seem to be pretty carefully selected; in part at least the marriages must serve economic and political ends and this in turn implies that the groom, though lower in rank, is probably a wealthy or influential person[5]. Nevertheless, the fact that a woman may marry a man of lower rank is undeniable and it is in this respect that the Katchin differ from the Batak. Leach's assumption that a Batak woman may marry a man of lower rank is not sufficiently supported by fact. Although wife-givers are superior

5 See also the interesting analysis by Luc de Heusch (1971, 116 ff.).

to wife-takers and wife-takers have to render services to their wife-givers, the status-difference is not generalized into a difference in rank. In effect, marriages are concluded between members of groups of equal social rank. Moreover, if a woman should marry a man of lower social rank, this would run counter to the fairly general principle of Indonesian marriage customs which very strictly forbids such marriages, whereas marriages between men of higher and women of lower rank are permitted.

We must maintain the conclusion that hypergamy is of frequent occurrence, whereas marriages between women of higher and men of lower rank are relatively rare. It is exactly the reverse of what could have been expected on the basis of the gift-theory and there is every reason to reconsider the logic underlying the custom. First of all we must point out that in societies where hypergamy occurs it is not the hypergamous marriages which are important; as it is, they are relatively rare, the great majority of the women marrying men of equal rank. The point is that no woman is permitted to marry a man of lower rank. The notion that the loss of a woman can be substituted with goods does not enter into the picture; it is a matter of the honour of the woman and her family. If the thesis that women are objects among other valuable goods were correct, there would be no explanation for the fact that people are so emotional about a girl marrying a man on a lower step of the social ladder. The most contradictory point of all is that the males who are more intent on upward social mobility than the females, promote the social mobility of the latter and deny themselves the possibility of upgrading by means of an ambitious marriage. The opportunities for upward social mobility are greater for women than for men. In this respect the women are not at all treated as objects; they are the repositories of the honour of the family and of greater importance than any goods. When a girl marries a groom of higher rank it is she who is promoted, her brothers contenting themselves with the glory reflecting from their relation to the woman and her husband. The advantage they derive from the transaction springs from her advancement in the social sphere, and the advancement of the sister is important enough to the brothers to make them willing to pay a dowry, thus reversing altogether the notion that women can be substituted for goods. The assumption that women are objects leads to insoluble contradictions. These can only be solved by assuming that the women behave as objects and that they do not agree to do so unless on their own conditions, one of these being that the brothers defend their honour, i.e. that they be recognized as the repositories of their families' honour. They are willing to behave as objects, provided these objects are acknowledged to be the most precious items imaginable, the symbols of the honour of the family. Wherever people are sensitive to social rank, a woman is not readily going to marry beneath her social status, except under special conditions.

Here, however, a problem arises. Marrying upwards the bride ascends to a more dignified status, but she loses her brother's protection. Brothers are incapable of protecting her against their social superiors. The consequences can be detrimental to the woman. Wolf, in his recent analysis of Chinese traditional marriage-forms, points out that a son's marriage with a woman of lower social status shields the family from intervention by the new wife's relatives if she should happen to have complaints – as she is only too likely to –

about her mother-in-law's demeanour (1968 p. 870). Hypergamy is an effective means of combining the satisfaction of the pride of the bride and her family with a strict curtailment of the latter's influence. Structurally, the situation is interesting; it highlights another aspect of the unsuitability of marrying a groom of lower social rank. The combination of lower social rank with the position of bride-taker would reduce the latter to an unbearable position of inferiority. Another important aspect is that of the authority pattern within the family. Authority is normally vested in the husband and this might be endangered if the wife were of higher rank. The solution of all these problems is to take a bride of equal or lower rank. The latter case is the one of hypergamy which has its special attractions: the bride is honoured, the brother improves his social status and pays for the honour with a dowry for his sister, while the husband and his family consolidate their independence of the bride-givers. Everybody stands to gain, at least formally, though to us the bride, who is the great winner, must appear to be the loser in the material sense, and her husband, socially the loser, the winner. Yet, this is only seemingly true because we appreciate the position of the bride as that of the newly married wife, unprotected amidst a family of strangers and under the strict supervision of a rancorous mother-in-law. This is not as the bride sees it; her perspective is necessarily that of her own motherhood, the mother of a son of rank.

Readers well acquainted with the œuvre of Lévi-Strauss will have noted that the argument developed in the previous pages is based on exactly the same notion of elementary forms of kinship as the one forwarded by Lévi-Strauss in his essay of 1945, *l'Analyse struc-*

turale en linguistique et en anthropologie (1958, ch. II).
A different appreciation of the brother-sister relationship led us to conclusions which deviate from those
arrived at by Lévi-Strauss on two important points.
In another field of enquiry, however, his views are
confirmed, viz. in that of the prevalence of the matrilateral cross-cousin marriage over other forms of cross-
cousin marriage. Approaching the subject from the
female point-of-view the first thing to note is that, to
a woman, marrying a father's sister's son (as she has
to do in matrilateral cross-cousin marriage) has the
advantage that the opportunities of her brother and
mother's brother to give her and her children the
protection they need, stand unimpaired. Her marriage
with a mother's brother's son, however, is less satisfactory. Her mother's brother, before her marriage,
is a protector, at least so in a patrilineal society; in a
matrilineal one his role is more authoritarian and all
we have to say on the disadvantages involved in marrying a mother's brother's son applies even more
strongly in a matrilineal society. As a consequence of
his niece's marrying his son the mother's brother turns
into an authority as well. The two functions need not
conflict with each other, but if they do the situation
affects her brother's opportunities to protect her. Her
father-in-law is also his mother's brother, a circumstance which limits his freedom of action in case of
conflict. Evidently, a conflict in a marriage between
a father's sister's daughter and a mother's brother's
son leads to greater complications than it would in a
marriage between a mother's brother's daughter and a
father's sister's son.

Finally, there is the possibility of bilateral cross-
cousin marriage. In its schematized ideal form it is a
marriage in which a brother and a sister marry a

sister and brother. In this form it is of extremely rare occurrence (if it occurs at all) and small wonder because it leads to a complete merging of all functions and to the ultimate isolation of the two families concerned from the society at large. In actual practice bilateral cross-cousin marriage is always, as Lévi-Strauss has cogently demonstrated, a marriage with either a matrilateral or a patrilateral cross-cousin because of the two marriages at least one is contracted between distant cross-cousins (1949 pp. 489 ff.). The conclusion is valid that from the women's standpoint the matrilateral variant of cross-cousin marriage is preferable to the patrilateral one, a conclusion which does not detract in any way from the value of Lévi-Strauss's argument that matrilateral cross-cousin marriage leads to an arrangement of social relations of greater structural perfection, a conclusion which should stand unimpaired.

It is worthwhile to extend the analysis to marriages between parallel cousins as well. Such marriages are fairly rare generally. This is not without reason because more often than not these are marriages between members of one and the same local descent-group. Nevertheless, marriages with a father's brother's daughter do occur. In many Arab societies they are even the rule, notwithstanding the prevailing patrilineal kinship structure. I also recorded this marriage-form among the Sasak of Lombok (Indonesia), although not as a general rule but rather as an expedient to avoid the expenses connected with a marriage between unrelated young people. Confining ourselves to patrilineal societies and societies with a patrilineal bias, we formulate the following hypothesis: as marrying a member of one's own local descent-group has the disadvantage of limiting the number and the extent of affinal relations, we may expect in patrilineal or patrilineally biased societies more marriages between matrilateral than between patrilateral parallel cousins. Curiously enough, the hypothesis is all wrong. Marriages between matrilateral parallel cousins are significantly fewer than between patrilateral parallel cousins. Why?

Again an explanation can be found by examining the case from the women's point of view. To them a marriage with either kind of parallel cousin is unattractive, though there is a difference in degree. Marrying a patrilateral parallel cousin the wife-to-be practically loses the protection of her brother because her husband and her brother are as brothers to each other. However, her maternal uncle's position remains unimpaired. Moreover, the marriage with a father's brother's son has the advantage that the woman continues to live in her own family compound. It is true that she enters another household, but that is about all there is to it. Marrying a mother's sister's son has none of these attractions. Normally the girl must take leave of her family of origin. The protection which her brother can give is again restricted as sister's sons, too, are as brothers to each other, though probably not to the same degree as brother's sons. In this respect the situation is slightly better, but the effect is completely cancelled out by the fact that she and her husband have one and the same mother's brother. The latter is under fully equal obligations to both, obligations which compete the one with the other in case of conflict between the spouses. What is worse, the relationship between sister's son and mother's brother tends to be closer and more affectionate than that between sister's daughter and mother's brother. In other words, the woman forfeits the protection of her mother's brother when she marries her mother's sister's son.

Our final conclusion is that the recognition of the women's part in the marriage trade leads to a sounder appreciation of the basic structures and principles of kinship. The pivotal significance of the brother-sister relationship has been clearly demonstrated, and so has the structural necessity of the influential role of the mother's brother. Another important conclusion is that wherever virilocal marriage is the rule, a bilineal system of kinship reckoning is latently implied. The system need not be made explicit but the two lines of descent are discerned and recognized anyhow, with or without making terminological distinctions explicit. We were also enabled to reconcile the contradictions connected with hypergamy. The reverse, marriage between a woman of high rank and a man of low rank, is virtually impossible because it would reduce the husband to a state of abject dependency. The only way to bridge the gap between groups of different rank is hypergamy. And, finally, the examination of the structural implications between cousins of different kind provided a valuable check of the validity and applicability of our approach.

One point still has to be made. The gift of a woman is a gift of a different character from that of valuables, however precious. A woman is not given as an object among other objects, she is part of a family and the symbol of its honour and presence. Even though behaving as an object, she is not really an object and never can be one, because her activities as a housewife and a mother in the new household continue to forge a never ending chain of debts owed by her husband to her brother and, as long as these activities continue, by her brother to her.

III

The role of women as care-givers

An analysis like the one presented in the previous paper, *The Part of Women in the Marriage Trade,* is not an analysis of directly observed reality, but of models constructed on the basis of a restricted number of variables derived from observed reality. A model does not tell us how or what reality is, but how and what a reality is like that does not contain other elements than those included in the model. Observable reality ordinarily (if not always) includes a variety of elements not foreseen in the models applied to it, a fact that does not detract from the value of models as heuristic devices, but simply reflects the limits of their applicability, limits defined by the factors included in the model.

A typical case of the impact of other factors on the validity of a model is that of the marriage relations in two New Guinea highlands communities which I propose to examine from the point of view of our model of the marriage trade. I selected them for discussion for yet another reason, the circumstance that the relevant ethnographic descriptions give extensive information on one of the main variables of our model, the function of women as care-givers. It is this function by which women, at their marriage the objects in the exchange consolidating the relations between groups of men, become the influential subjects who, imperceptibly, weave the web of restrictions and inhibitions curtailing the apparent freedom of their males. The contradictions inherent to the position of women have their counterpart in those pertinent to the situation of the males. The sexes are complementary to one another, and it is impossible to understand the position of the women without paying due attention to that of the men. An analysis of the data derived from a few well observed cases can contribute substantially to a more realistic appreciation of the fact that the position of one of the sexes in a society is necessarily a function of that of the other, and *vice versa*.

The first of the two ethnographic descriptions to which, in the first part of this paper, I wish to draw the readers' attention, is concerned with married life in the Mount Hagen area in New Guinea, Marilyn Strathern's book *Women in Between; Female Roles in a Male World* (1972). It gives a penetrating analysis of the ambiguous position of a married woman: on the one hand she is a wife, the life-companion of her husband, to whose family she is an outsider; and on the other hand she is a sister and daughter, a member of her own lineage and subclan, yielded to her husband for the purpose of creating or maintaining an affinal bond, a lasting alliance with another subclan, a valuable relation in an unsafe world, ridden by warfare. She is in-between in every respect, not really trusted by her husband's people before she has borne him a couple of children and has proved her worth generally, ordinarily little protected by her own kin unless protection holds a promise of future gain. At the same time the married woman is immensely valuable to both sides; to her husband because he gave bride-wealth for her in the expectation of children, labour, and household-care; to her own kin who have a keen interest in the success of her marriage because it must warrant the recurrent exchange of pigs and valuables, and function as a basis for alliance in times of war. To her family of origin the possibility that the marriage might have to be dissolved and the bride-price returned because of her misbehaviour, is as real a threat as the possibility of her secretly conspiring against her husband's subclan is to her in-laws. Being in-between is a difficult position. Those women who take things as they are and know how to manipulate the various opportunities implied in an ambiguous situation, get away with it. For many of them the problem is too much; the high incidence of suicide among married women holds a clear indication that a successful solution of their problems is too arduous a task for many of them, notably for those who are partners in a polygynous household. Relations between co-wives ordinarily are strained and a source of recurring conflicts.

In most respects the facts comply with the model presented in the previous essay, but there are two exceptions. The first is that the lot of Mount Hagen women is harder than the model suggests, the great stumbling-block being polygyny. Polygyny is a privilege that only the rich and the powerful can afford, a token of wealth. The institution is clearly associated with male supremacy over women. The women dislike it but submit, be it unwillingly. Apparently they see no other way out.

The second exception is that mother's brother, though an important relative for his sister's son, is not so for her daughter. The obvious explanation is that the relation between uncle and nephew is dominated by their exchange-relationship, a feature of particular interest in a society consistently divided into mutually hostile clans and subclans to whom gift-exchange ceremonies are the exclusive instrument for peaceful contacts. As women do not partake in these ceremonies, at least not directly or openly, the mother's brother's affections naturally go to sister's son, not to her daughter. We shall later find that there is another and structurally more fundamental reason behind it. For the moment it must suffice that a woman must rely on her brother for protection, and on him alone. Although the relations between siblings of opposite sex are affectionate and close generally, the protection offered to the sister is too much a function of the material interests of her and her brother's subclan to be really efficient, at least in many cases.

The question arises why women so meekly follow the dictates of the men, willingly accepting the object-role assigned to them and, if the faithful fulfilment of that role leads to a thoroughly unhappy marriage, prefer individual suicide to communal resistance. It is not a question relevant to the Mount Hagen situation only. In various parts of the world a married woman's lot is a miserable one. The phenomenon is so wide-spread that observers often are inclined to take this more or less as a matter of course, the direct consequence of the superior physical force of the males. The explanatory value of this reference to the physical powers of the males is small. The women's contributions to the household economy and to household care generally are so substantial that fear for the physical force of the men is but a poor explanation for the women's readiness to submit to their extravagancies. If it ever came to fighting, women might well appear to be hardly as weak as they are supposed to be. They are better accustomed to hard and strenuous work than the men, and better trained to support themselves.

In many primitive societies 'dependent people' are more numerous among the men than among the women. If really unwilling the men would have a hard job to repress their women's rebellion.

Additional and enlightening information on the position of married women in the New Guinea highlands is presented by Hylkema in his description of a Nalum speaking group in a small valley just north of the Star Mountains (West-Irian). The author's intimate knowledge of the personal life histories of the mountaineers among whom he spent eight years as a missionary, enabled him better to assess many of their private motivations. His account is that of an attentive witness to the numerous conflicts pertaining to the social life of a small group whose life-conditions differ next to nothing from those of the Mount Hagen Papuans to whom they are culturally very similar. Here again, the mother's brother is of slight importance to sister's daughter, at least as far as protection goes. The relations between brother and sister, however, are close and intimate, perhaps closer than in Mount Hagen but this may be only seemingly so, because Nalum women are not so desparately in need of protection as their Mount Hagen sisters. Polygyny is relatively rare, and girls are more freely allowed to take the initiative in the choice of a husband than happens to be the case in the Mount Hagen area. The difference coincides with the more modest role of wealth and the exchange of valuables in this rather isolated community.

The fact that Nalum women are a little bit better off than those of Mount Hagen does not imply that their married life is a happy one generally. The contrary is true. A marriage often starts fairly well, but in the long run the partners tend to become alienated from each other, the husband orienting his life more and more on the men's house, the wife on her children and her garden. Reaching old age, the husband, more than ever associating himself with the men's house, sometimes depends upon the help of a daughter or of a son-in-law, the wife finding accomodation with one of her sons. Marriage relations slowly deteriorate, and so do family relations. The sons, a man's pride, grow up to become their father's competitors. Ultimately, they go their own way, breaking away from his authority. Old men are lonely, usually even more so than old women, although the latter's lot is not always an enviable one either. Normally, the story of a marriage is one of continued strife and conflict. An important source of conflict is alluded to in the title of Hylkema's book, *Mannen in het Draagnet*, Men in the Carrying-bag[1]. The carrying-bag is the net used by mothers for transporting their babies. The men feel themselves encapsulated by their women's cares. This does not mean that Nalum society is one in which the women dominate. Externally, and in many respects internally as well, social life is as patently male dominated as any Papuan society. Yet, the women have their way with it, and it is worth while to note how they have it.

The socially approved manner of arranging a marriage is that a father offers his daughter to a young man by bringing her to the latter's village to discuss the affair with the senior male relatives of the groom elect. Very often, in at least one half of the cases, another procedure is followed, one in which the girl has the initiative. One of the occasions for intervillage

[1] Unfortunately the book, edited in the Dutch language as nr. 67 of the Verhandelingen van het Koninklijk Instituut voor Taal-, Land- en Volkenkunde (1974), could not be translated into English.

contacts is noctural dance feasts. The dancers are the visiting young men, the spectators the people of the host village, the most interested onlookers being the girls. If one of the dancers takes her fancy, a girl secretly makes off before daybreak, often accompanied by another girl who has similar plans. They wait for the visiting party on its return to its own village, and explain the men whom of the boys each of them has chosen. They need not even know his name. Usually the boy accepts and the girl accompanies him to his village to face the often considerable problems that such a marriage by surprise may evoke. The point of interest is the eagerness of the girl to leave her village of origin. It is true that villages usually are small, exogamous subclan settlements that a girl must leave anyhow. But she need not leave it this way, taking the risk of binding herself to a husband whom she does not know at the price of grieving her own family, and of being met with resistance or even hostility by the groom's family who may have very different plans. A girl who does this must be firmly bent on making her own life. The risks are real and numerous; she may be sent back to her family, abused and chased away by the groom's mother, or forced to make a second choice among the boys of the village.

However contracted, initially a marriage may have its proper romance. The girl, the more resolute of the two, may even persuade her young husband to construct a house outside the village where she can have him for herself alone. In the course of rarely more than a few years they will settle in his village. She has to yield him to his own men's house, gradually but consistently, until over the years he will reside more or less permanently in the men's house, for a long time still enjoying his meals at his wife's house or taking them to the men's house, until, at last, he prepares many of his own meals there.

In the mean time there are children. Women want to have children, preferably sons. If a boy is born, the mother welcomes him saying: 'Don't weep, my dear, I am going to give you my breast. When you are grown up and my husband an old man, you will fence in my garden'. If the newly born is a girl, she speaks differently: 'come, my dear, I am going to give you my breast. Yet, I will welcome the day on which they marry you off to a distant valley'. Further inquiries confirmed that both forms of addressing a baby are common usage (Hylkema 1974 pp. 202 f.). Thus three points are clear: the woman's strong support of the rules of local exogamy and virilocal marriage, her concentration on her son, and her devotion to her economic preoccupation, gardening. Of the latter little more can be said than that her economic role is a woman's basic legitimation in society. A woman is judged by her domestic capabilities, primarily those of devotion to gardening.

Her relations to her son are more complicated. As long as the son is unmarried he can be sure that his mother will provide him with food. Trouble starts when he wishes to marry, either because a girl is offered to him by her father, or because a girl selected him by following him to his village. Altogether too often the mother resists, threatening alternately to kill either him or her, or preparing to commit suicide. More than once she succeeds in dissuading her son from marrying that particular girl, but in the long run she invariably is the loser. For a time the relations between mother and son are strained or even broken up, but finally she will acquiesce and reconcile herself to the inevitable and to her son who, when she is old, will be her refuge on whom she relies.

I shall not dwell on further details. The main point is the woman's concentration on her care-giving role. This role is her monopoly. It is, of course, a natural role as far as infants are concerned, but the role is extended socially (and culturally) to include her husband and grown-up sons, not to her grown-up daughters who are care-givers in their own right and thus no longer objects of care to the mother, but potential competitors. What a woman is after, at least in Nalum society, is to find herself a unit in which she is the main care-giver, a unit all of her own to realize her care-giving passions. This makes it attractive to her to break away from her parents to acquire a husband all for herself, and to have sons to care for when her husband withdraws himself from her often too obtrusive succour. The close relations between brothers and sisters make it desirable to have the daughters married off to a distant valley. Otherwise they might altogether too easily become the mother's competitors. In other words, not the men but the women are the real supporters of the prevailing system of virilocal marriage and local exogamy. The system implies that mothers' brothers give support to their sisters' sons, but not to their sisters' daughters. The sons are the real objects of their mothers' cares, not the daughters. The sons also are their mothers' security; they will support her when she is old. Close relations between a mother's brother and his sister's daughter could only upset the system which refers the daughter to a (more) distant valley, an objective that easily wins the support of the males who have an interest in exchange relations with more distant communities.

All this holds true for the Mount Hagen people as

well. In Mrs. Strathern's account we find very little on the relations between mother and daughter, but much on those between mother and son. A mother even continues to provide her son with food after he has already married (M. Strathern 1972 p. 20). The basic pattern is the same, but the position of Mount Hagen women is weaker. They do not fight as resolutely as Nalum women do to secure themselves a private unit to care for. Apparently, Mount Hagen women are too valuable; loose conduct of a girl can have an unfavourable effect on the bride-price that can be asked for her. Therefore she is chaperoned by her mother when she attends a dance-feast, and cannot permit herself the freedom that a Nalum girl enjoys. Instead of contributing to their independence, the high value set on women results in less freedom and more unhappiness. The greater value of the women is defined by purely male interests, alliances in war, and exchange partners for the accumulation of wealth.

I must leave aside to what extent a closer relationship between mother's brother and sister's son than between him and her daughter, is of more general occurrence. The question is of interest, but cannot be discussed without comparing a diversity of cultures. Instead, I shall return to our initial question, why women so meekly submit to the extravagancies of the males. It is a question that has a bearing on really very many societies and cultures. Therefore we must return to the women's self-selected role of care-giving. It refers straightaway to the women's nurturing function, a function based in nature. It is women who bear children. They are equipped with special glands for nurturing a baby during the first year of its life. Satisfying the need to empty the lacteal glands gives the young mother a sense of physical well-being. The physiological evidence suggests the probability that a woman's physical constitution has an effect of some sort on her behavioral make-up, enough at least to induce personal satisfaction in nurturing and in care-giving generally. However, it is by no means certain that this results directly from her physiological condition, because in each and every culture the education of girls is deliberately geared to the successful performance of future motherhood. From early age onwards a girl is conditioned to care-giving as her final destination. We are treading here the borderland between nature and culture where it is difficult to discern what is innate from what is the effect of learning. Yet, the female bent toward nurturing her babies is sufficiently general for us to presume an inner disposition that is strong enough to be culturally developed into an inclination to care-giving, an inclination that is so wide-spread that it is almost a universal.

It is this inclination, however developed culturally, that makes women immensely valuable to society in general, and to men in particular. For a man life without the succour of a woman is hard to bear (cf. Lévi-Strauss 1949, p. 46). It is she who collects vege-table food, insects and molluscs, she also who prepares them. Moreover, she can be expected to give comfort in misfortune and pain. On the other hand, she can extend her cares too far, trying to encapsulate her husband with her attentions in order to have him for herself alone. The care-giving passion that makes women valuable, also can make them a nuisance. What is worse, it makes them vulnerable. Their passion strongly binds women to the objects of their cares, and many women are prepared to go to any length to safeguard these ties, even to the extent of accepting a co-wife or the position of a concubine. The position of a wife is the exact counterpart of the style of her care-giving, always vacillating between two poles: that of the exertion of power by encapsulation, and that of submission in mere servitude.

The specialization of women on care-giving in a small unit, necessarily the family-unit, defines the position of the men. The objects of their wives' cares, the men turn outward, to occupations outside the narrow family circle in which the more important functions are the prerogative of women. Breaking away from their wives' cares, the men seek the company of other men, living in similar conditions as they, to pursue ends that give satisfaction to their own strivings for power or dominance. Materially cared for by their wives, the men have time and opportunity to devote themselves to other pursuits than hunting or fishing only. We find them engaged in ritual, war, and gift-exchange, frequently consulting together and busily planning schemes for ever new activities when assembled in those strongholds of male 'apartheid', the men's house or the ceremonial grounds.

In all this there is hardly anything that is new, and the reader who accuses me of stressing the obvious has sound reason to feel justified. Nevertheless, I wonder whether it really is as obvious as it should be. A case in point is that of our old, male-biased theories on human origins. Although most of them have been refuted on many grounds, it is doubtful whether the old bias has been rejected with them. It is true enough that we have given up the belief in the polygamous and jealous father of the primeval horde who drove out his sons in order to keep the women, his wives and daughters, all to himself. The theory, a masterpiece of male pride, was developed by early anthropologists to explain the origin of exogamy, and applied by Freud in support of his theory of the Oedipus-complex. It was falsified on various grounds, but not one of these grounds referred to the ominous fact that the model of the horde ascribes all action and every change to the males and to the males only. Ignoring the women, socially disapproved as rude, does not give offence in scientific theory. The theory of the horde by now being obsolete, we might argue that the issue should be forgotten. However, the issue as such is still actual. We need at least some notion of what the life of early man was like. The development of modern ethology has given a new sense of actuality to this need. What are the elements that a hypothetical model of early human society should contain?

The jealous father chasing his sons can, by now, be ruled out. We never came across a single case of it in known history. Sons are the arrows in the father's quiver everywhere (Ps. 127 : 4, 5). Unfortunately, thus far no one ever gave serious thought to the possibility of reversing the expulsion scheme by hypothesizing that it was not the father who turned out his sons, but the mother who sent off her daughters. And yet, there is solid ground for it in what still happens today. We need only remember the Nalum mother expressing the wish that her daughter shall be married off to a distant valley as early as possible. And of course she wishes; holding the monopoly of care-giving in the family-group, it is sheer logic that she fears the competition of a grown-up daughter. We are entitled to suppose that a mother in early human society addressed her daughter more or less in the following vein: 'you slut, find yourself a boy-friend elsewhere, but not here with your brothers and father! Get out from here!' It is not necessary to suppose that a scene of this kind led to physical violence or immediate expulsion, to recognize the inner consistency of the mother-daughter conflict with the social pattern of group life in a society where the mother has a monopoly of care-giving. Is there any probability that the mother held such a monopoly in early human society?

The hypothesis may seem surprising, but it certainly is pretty near to what we know today of primate behaviour, considerably nearer than that of the jealous father. Thus we know now that chimpansees stay with their mother for years on end, till well into adolescence. They have no fathers supervising them. Although there are respected older males in the troop, these do not exercise father-functions, and they are not committed to a female by special ties resembling a marriage relation or anything alike it. In fact, there is sound reason for this; female chimpansees are sexually accessible only once in two years for a two weeks' period, a period too short for developing behavioral patterns of sexual exclusivity. It seems that, in this respect, other primates are not very much different (cf. Jolly 1972, ch. 10-13). Human females are the great exception in nature, sexually accessible all the year round. This makes them extremely attractive to human males, attractive enough for them to moderate their promiscuous desires and to give in to the females' preference for each a special male of her own.

This preference is, of course, hypothesis, but a hypothesis that has probability. The extreme helplessness of the human baby and the excessively long period of dependence during childhood suggest a disposition of the mother toward care-giving, a disposition supported by her capacity of prolonged lactation. Care-giving implies a certain devotion to an object, primarily a child but not necessarily a child only. In as far as it is a more or less fixed behavioral pattern, it can be extended to any object. Moreover, the male, having been cared for until well into adolescence, is well acquainted with female care. Besides, the males need not surrender to their females' wishes in every respect. Unrestrained by a special inclination towards care-giving and nurturing the males do not give up their roving habits. Their greater physical prowess makes them better fit than women for mobile habits and aggressive occupations, such as hunting. A division of labour between the sexes by which hunting readily becomes a male occupation, is natural, the female altogether too often being curtailed in her freedom of movement by the presence of infants. Hunting also enables the male to prove his worth to his female and to ingratiate himself with her by sharing his catch. At the same time hunting favours the male's association with other males, an association which, in time, enables him to make the best of his consort's wish to be rid of her (and his) daughters at the earliest possible convenience by offering these daughters to his fellow-men. Yet, adolescent daughters are not will-less creatures, and adolescent sons are not either. They grew up together and are attached to each other, so much so that the mother feels that she has to send her daughters away. We know what the outcome is, the marriage trade as analyzed in the previous essay. The exact history of its development is unknown, but the model just described contains all the elements that are necessary to explain the result as we know it. The model even explains the ease by which women let themselves be made the objects of exchange transactions between groups of men.

In this hypothesis no mention is made of protection, nor of the widely accepted supposition that marriage ties are necessary because a female is in need of protection and assistance every time that a birth immobilizes her for a couple of months during which she has to give all her time and attention to the newly born baby. This is not an omission. The model does not need this element. Protection can and will be given by the combined males of a troop or group anyway. It is more effective than the protection proffered by an individual husband. Protection is consequent upon group membership, not on individual marriage relations that are implied. Moreover, husband and wife do not often forage in each other's company. In the morning the men go out hunting together, whilst the women set out, usually in another direction, to collect vegetable food together. They will meet again in camp at some time in the afternoon.

It is different with assistance. This is a young mother's specific and urgent need during the first months of her baby's life. However, the kind of assistance needed is sex-specific; another must perform the duties that ordinarily fall to the woman, the collection of vegetable food, the preparation of food, and keeping an eye on the other children. These tasks can better be attended to by another woman than by a man, even if this man be a husband. In fact, every woman has her deputies. If she has to absent herself for a shorter or longer time, there is always an aunt willing to take care of a baby or to look after the infants and children. This even happens in a troop of primates (Jolly 1972 pp. 251 ff.). Why should this have been different in early human society? Do we find anywhere that a young father is of great help in his household just after a baby has been born? Is not his first concern to worry about finding female assistance if such assistance is not already present? This is, actually, what happens in any culture.

We conclude that all this talk of protection and the need women have of it, is just another myth. The protection given by the men is given communally, not individually. The myth must have been invented by women to lure men into marriage, into willingness to submit themselves to their loving cares. It suits the lover's role as well as that of the care-giving mother to make the man believe that she needs him badly. The men easily fall for it; it enhances their feelings of self-esteem and they like to hear it again and again. The myth, having a basis in reality, the protection communally given, is readily believed by men and women alike; as Aldous Huxley said, somewhere in *Brave New World*: sixty six thousand repetitions make one truth.

We have considered the position of women from the point of view of 'Women in Between', of 'Female roles in a male World'. By now it is time to reverse the approach and to examine the male roles in a female world by considering the position of Men in Between. To that end we have to start from the fact that women are (potential) mothers. It is the perspective in which girls see themselves in practically every culture (cf. Mead 1949 pp. 81 ff.) with the possible exception of modern civilization where it is unethical for a woman to have all the children she might wish to have since modern science offers effective protection against untimely death. The problems ensuing from progress and modern development, however, should not here be made the object of our concern. Really interesting for our present purposes are the reactions of the males to the cares bestowed on them by the women.

These reactions are ambiguous. On the one hand the women's cares are accepted as a right, appreciated as good and even as pleasant. But at the same time they are resented and rejected as efforts on the women's side to encapsulate them, to tie them with apron-strings. The resentment creates a fertile soil for the always present suspicions aroused by the twofold loyalties of the manipulating women, the one to their husbands, the other to their own kin, especially their brothers who, as mothers' brothers to the children, have many, too many opportunities to meddle in family-affairs. The men react by creating a distance between themselves and the women. There are male affairs and female affairs, and the division of labour easily develops into an instrument of antagonism between the sexes, an antagonism institutionalized in clubs, men's houses, and secret rituals. These institutions are wide-spread and have many forms. Their importance was recognized as early as 1902 by Heinrich Schurtz. The men do not content themselves with having their own rituals and club-houses, often they even use these rituals to frighten the women into subservience and to compel them to serve their husbands with festive meals. But is this presentation of the facts by Schurtz (in his *fin-de-siècle* outlook a male among males himself) all that can be said of it? We should have a closer look at the procedures followed in these fright-instilling rituals.

Of course, the women are not really attacked; they are chased off by frightening them. A favoured instrument to warn them off is the bullroarer. As soon as its shrieking sound is heard, the women know that they have to clear out. Screaming for fright they run away, believing that the noise is the voice of a demon. That is what the men told them, and believe that they believe. But do they really? Although there is no reason to doubt that they believe that something uncanny is at hand, there is ample evidence that in many cases the women know exactly how the noise is produced. Another point of interest is that there are always women present at the moment that they must be frightened off. Moreover, they duly return as soon as the men have something spectacular to show that must be seen and admired. A recurring feature in the descriptions of Australian initiation ceremonies is that the women alternately play a part and make off or stay away until it is their turn again to participate. Obviously, there is close cooperation, warranting that the ritual proceeds smoothly. In truth, even the scenes in which the women run off, screaming for fright at the voice of the bullroarer, are real contributions to the success of the ritual. The men who handle the bullroarers are inclined to take the noise anything but seriously. This is a bad thing in itself, because a ritual that is not taken seriously has no sense and no psychological effect. The women, by being frightened, help to persuade their teasers that there is something in it anyhow. The frightened women, acting as true believers, contribute immensely to the sense of reality that every ritual badly needs. They do the same when, after long preparations, the men are ready to show themselves to the women and the latter reward them with signs of awe and admiration, a really touching case being that of the descent of the *hevehe* masks described by F. E. Williams in his *Drama of Orokolo*.

In all this the women keep true to their role of care-givers, encouraging their husbands and sons to pursue the ends that have taken their imagination. This co-operation, however, does not take away the antagonism that persists, and finds the most diverse expressions.

Outstanding among these are the manifestations of male ideas concerning fertility. They are of specific interest in this context because fertility is a female specialty, the contributions of the males being, in fact, of minor importance. Nevertheless, the latter cherish the idea that, in one way or another, the men are the mainspring of fertility. Not satisfied with the pleasure of the sexual act alone, they wish to be important by emphasizing the significance of their contributions to their wives' fertility, and even to fertility in general, by making fertility one of the principal aims of their rituals. It is not simply sexual envy on the part of the males; their envy of female fertility is only one aspect of an inferiority complex that has a solid ground in economic reality. The men are unimportant economically; in the previous essay we argued that the great contributors to the household economy are the women, their share in the acquisition of food calories amounting to more than twice of that of the men. In the great civilizations – China, India, the Middle East, Europe – the men made good by making themselves important economically, a development that enabled them to realize their sex-antagonism by confining their women to the household. In primitive society the men have to find compensation in their rituals, and this is one of the main reasons why women cannot have more than a minor share in them. Ritual activity tends to be a male monopoly.

One might object that all this does not hold true for the Australians. They deny that the sexual act has any effect on conception. Pregnancy is ascribed to a totem-ancestor's action of sending a germ of life into the woman's womb. Sexual intercourse being degraded to a pleasurable act only, the power of fertility seems to be recognized as primarily a female

116

prerogative. It is not. It is the male ancestors who are the real fertilizers, and this leads us back to the men who, by means of their rituals, induce the totem-ancestors to perform their beneficent activities. There is no question of real ignorance of the meaning of the sexual act in the Australian case. Some twelve years ago I argued at some length that the Australian cults are primarily phallic cults (Van Baal 1963). I shall not repeat the argument and restrict myself to what I hold to be the most impressive case, that of the *Engwura*-ceremony as described by Spencer and Gillen (1927 vol. I ch. X f.). Toward the end of the rites, the myth of the great Achilpa-ancestor is re-enacted. The chief, impersonating the ancestor whose reincarnation he is, sits down with in front of his belly a phallic object that he moves up and down with his hands, an activity in which he is assisted by two other old men, sitting to his right and left. The two other men impersonate the ancestor's wives, and the scene refers to his life-producing activities, projecting *kuruna*, life-germs, into his two wives from a pouch called *ambilia ekura* that he carried with him. *Ambilia ekura* is also the name given to the phallic object that the chief moves up and down in front of his belly. The meaning of the name is, literally, baby-bag, and is, 'in fact, the name actually given to the bag, really the amnion in which the unborn child lies within its mother' (Spencer & Gillen 1927 I, p. 225). The ritual scene is a symbolic copulation, but the real point of interest is that the phallus, the penis, is identified with an amnion, a womb. The ultimate source of fertility is the males.

Other peoples more openly claim that all fertility stems from the males. The Marind-anim of South New Guinea are a case in point (cf. Van Baal 1966, more in particular pp. 162 ff., 948 ff.). Of course, they do not deny that it is the women who become pregnant and bear the children, but they contend that this is unimportant in view of what the men do to it, namely making them pregnant. Nothing would come out of it, if the men did not exert themselves to copulate many times with them and, at a ceremony held to celebrate either a marriage or the end of a period of continence due to lactation, to do the same in cooperation with many men who, one after another, have intercourse with the woman who is the object of their combined efforts at fertilization. The ceremony is called *dom-bombari*, bad rite, a name reflecting how homosexuals think about it (*ibid.* p. 951). Male homosexuality is strongly institutionalized in Marind-anim society. It is positively valued, associated with the moiety connected with the more favourable aspects of their universe and with the leadership of the great, central rituals, whereas heterosexuality belongs to the moiety associated with the bad season, sorcery, war (headhunting) and the celebration of the big, public festivities.

Male homosexuality is, of course, a repudiation of the female sex, like, in a more moderate way, the segregation of the sexes in men's and women's houses. One may expect that this had a detrimental effect on married life, and, indeed, we found a remarkably low fertility rate, next to (relatively vague) indications that the sexual life of the Marind-anim, in spite of its intensity, was unsatisfactory to both sexes. Nevertheless, married life was by no means as poor as, for example, among the Mountain Papuans described earlier in this paper. Marriage bonds were lasting, and married couples often lived in fairly good comradeship until well into old age. Another surprising feature is the share that women were permitted to have in the performance of the secret rituals (with the exception, of course, of the homosexual rites).

Marind-anim ritual abounds with contradictory references to the female sex, some of them highly significant. Thus we find that the word *kuma*, *i.e.* what is ritually secret, is also used figuratively for the female genital (*ibid.* pp. 930 f.). In spite of the overt emphasis on male superiority, the real secret of the central ritual is that a female goddess is paramount, the Old Woman of the *mayo*-ritual of the eastern Marind, and of the *imo*-ritual of the mid-western. In the *mayo*-ritual she appears in two different forms, as the mother carrying the neophytes into the ceremonial grounds where they will stay for months on end, and as the mythical sister of the crocodile, married to the prominent representative of sun and coconut, whom she kept caught in copulation until, after a long time, the man was set free by force. In both qualities the *Mayo*-Woman is personified by a man. In the final rites, celebrating the deliverance of the male hero from embrace in copulation, the Old Woman, now symbolically represented by an equally symbolic snake, will be killed and annihilated. In the *imo*-ritual the threatening aspects of the Old Woman are even more emphatic. Here she is given the surname of Excrement Woman, a goddess of death and decay, personified by a man who is the effective (though not the official) master of the rites.

A curious feature of the *Mayo*-Woman is her appearance in yet another guise. This takes place in the context of the mourning ceremonies held in commemoration of a recently deceased initiate, always a grown-up man. One morning the women go in procession to visit the various spots frequented by the deceased during his lifetime. The procession is headed by a young woman in festive attire. She personifies the mythical *Mayo*-Woman. The dialectics of the *Mayo*-Woman's manifestations are intriguing. In the life-giving central ritual she is alternately a mother and a dangerous woman, threatening the male with castration. In both functions she is personified by a man. In the mourning ceremonies, however, she is a young and attractive woman, expressing her pity for the deceased's fate and serving his ghost with titbits of food and betelnut that the accompanying women scatter on the spots where he used to linger. We note that the dangerous, old woman, personified by a man, is how the men see the *Mayo*-Woman, the young and compassionate woman, personified by a woman, how the women see her.

A more comprehensive account of the contrarieties characterizing the image of the female in Marind-anim myth and ritual would exceed the scope of this paper by far. The point of interest is the convincing evidence that the males have to pay for their repudiation of the females. In myth and ritual they grudgingly admit the female's superiority, at the same time expressing their fears of being encapsulated in a variety of myths elaborating on the theme of castration anxiety. The Marind-anim are not the only people with problems of this kind. The Mount Hagen men who succeeded so well in subduing their women, celebrate a cult of the female spirit. The female spirit is a young and beautiful woman who gives fertility, but she has no genital (Andr. Strathern 1970). Subconsciously, the men know altogether too well how and where they are caught and encapsulated. They resist and try to retrieve an illusory independence by rewarding their women's cares with harsh treatment and exclusion from the rites. It is all in vain; the men realize too well how much advantage they take of their women's services. Again and again they have to recognize female superiority in myth and ritual, in which the effects of a bad conscience are plainly manifest. Sometimes they are veiled by the forbidding reifications of female dangerousness, but often the injustice done to their women is openly confessed in myths ascribing the origin of the cult and the cultus implements to women. A telling case is that of the myth of the Djanggawul-sisters of northeastern Arnhem Land (Warner 1958; R. Berndt, 1952).

The sisters are real culture-heroes; they give shape to the landscape, they produce the (phallic!) ritual implements, they initiate the ritual, and they give birth to many boys and girls. There is also a brother, but his role is a minor one, although not really unimportant. One day the men, headed by the brother, take possession of the ritual implements and start the ritual whilst the sisters are fishing. They are soon aware of it, but cannot interfere because they know the secret power of the sacred songs and fear to do anything about it. The older sister is the first to realize the consequences of what happened; resigning in her fate she states:

' 'Men can do it now, they can look after it. We can spend our time collecting bush foods for them ... We know everything. We have really lost nothing, for we remember it all, and we let them have that small part. For aren't we still sacred, even if we have lost the bags [with the sacred cult implements]? Haven't we still our uteri?' ' (Berndt 1952 pp. 40 f.).

The younger sister agrees. Together, the sisters are paragons of maturity. Yet, it is the men who tell the myth, tacitly admitting that the women, as superior mothers, let them, the boys, have their way. The women are sacred in their own right; they have their uteri, and the rebellious men cannot do without them. Like the women, the men too are 'in between', the captives of conflicting desires, the one to enjoy the cares and caresses of their women, the other to do as they like in complete freedom of the obligations ensuing from the rule of reciprocity, the golden rule for all interpersonal relations. The circumstance that, in the small family circle, reciprocity is necessarily of the informal kind, gives ample opportunity to an uneven distribution of charges and benefits between the sexes, an imbalance victimizing the married women because they are the central figures of the family circle. However, this does not mean that the 'golden rule' is essentially weak, permitting the men to go scot-free. The contrary is true; the rule is paramount and takes revenge on the wrong-doers by haunting them with all the afflictions of a bad conscience.

The relations between the sexes are a perennial problem, in modern times presenting itself in the obsessions of psychopathology, in primitive society in the disquieting metaphors of myth and ritual. It is not a matter of greater or lesser sexual freedom or of equal rights. The liberalisation of sexual morality enacted in the present century solved some problems and raised others. And equal rights are a matter of legislation, effective in public life but not in the domain where the real problems arise, that of the private life of two individuals of different sex. Fundamentally, the relations between the sexes are a structural problem, deeply rooted in the dialectics of the human condition, those of being subject opposed to and separate from the universe of which one makes part and belongs to. To be both part and subject and to be it always at the same time is a never ending and never completed task. It even is in that intimate relationship called marriage that, because of its complementary nature, holds the most favourable conditions for its fulfilment.

Bibliography

Ardrey, Robert
  1970 The Social Contract. Collins, Fontana Libr. References
        to 2nd. ed., 1972.
Baal, J. van
  1963 The Cult of the Bull-roarer in Australia and Southern
        New Guinea. *In*: Bijdragen tot de Taal-, Land- en
        Volkenkunde 119 : 201-214.
  1966 Dema; Description and Analysis of Marind-anim Cul-
        ture. The Hague, Nijhoff.
  1971 Symbols for Communication. Assen, Van Gorcum.
  1972 Pourquoi épouser le Marxisme? *In*: Bijdragen tot de
        Taal-, Land- en Volkenkunde 128: 118-126.
  1974 De Agressie der Gelijken. Assen, Van Gorcum.
  1975 De fenomenologie van Offer en Geschenk. *In*: Neder-
        lands Theologisch Tijdschrift 29: 1.
Berndt, Ronald M.
  1952 Djanggawul. London, Routledge & Kegan Paul.
Berndt, Ronald M. and Catherine H.
  1964 The World of the first Australians. Sydney, Ure Smith.
Blau, Peter M.
  1964 Exchange and Power in Social Life. New York, Wiley
        & Son.
Burridge, Kenelm
  1969 Tangu Traditions. Oxford, Clarendon Press.
Chabot, H. Th.
  1950 Verwantschap, Stand en Sexe in Zuid-Celebes. Gro-
        ningen-Djakarta, Wolters.
Cunnison, Ian
  1966 Marcel Mauss, The Gift. Translation. London, Cohen
        & West.

Davy, Georges
1922　La Foi Jurée. Paris, Félix Alcan.
Dewey, Alice G.
1962　Peasant Marketing in Java. Free Press of Glencoe.
Durkheim, Émile
1893　De la Division du Travail Social. Paris, Félix Alcan.
Evans-Pritchard, E. E.
1940　The Nuer. Oxford, Clarendon Press.
Gouldner, A. W.
1960　The Norm of Reciprocity; a preliminary Statement. *In*: American Sociological Review 25: 161-178.
Heusch, Luc de
1971　Pourquoi l'Épouser? et autres Essais. Éditions Gallimard.
Hiatt, L. R.
1964　Incest in Arnhem Land. *In*: Oceania 35: 124-128.
1966　A Spear in the Ear. *In*: Oceania 37: 153 f.
Hobbes, Thomas
1651　Leviathan, or the Matter, Form and Power of a Commonwealth. *In*: The English Works of Th. Hobbes, ed. Molesworth, 2nd Reprint. Aalen, Scientia Verlag, 1966.
Hoebel, E. Adamson
1954　The Law of primitive Man. Harvard University Press.
Hylkema o.f.m., S.
1974　Mannen in het Draagnet. Verhandelingen van het Koninklijk Instituut voor Taal-, Land- en Volkenkunde vol. 67. The Hague, Nijhoff.
Jolly, Alison
1972　The Evolution of Primate Behavior. New York, Mac-Millan.
Josselin de Jong, J. P. B. de
1952　Lévi-Strauss's Theory on Kinship and Marriage. Mededelingen van het Rijks Museum voor Volkenkunde, Leiden, nr. 10. Leiden, Brill.
Landtman, Gunnar
1927　The Kiwai Papuans of British New Guinea. London, MacMillan.
Leach, E. R.
1951　The structural Implications of matrilateral cross-cousin Marriage. *In*: Journal Royal Anthropological Institute 81: 23-55.
Lévi-Strauss, Claude
1949　Les Structures élémentaires de la Parenté. Paris, Presses

Universitaires de France. References to 2nd. edition: La Haye, Mouton, 1967.

1950   Introduction à l'Œuvre de Marcel Mauss. *In*: Mauss 1950: IX-LII.

1958   Anthropologie Structurale. Paris, Plon.

Maddock, Kenneth

1970   A structural Interpretation of the *Miriri*. *In*: Oceania 40: 165-176.

Mair, Lucy

1936   Chieftainship in modern Africa. *In*: Africa IX: 305-316.

Makarius, R.

1966   Incest and Redemption in Arnhem Land. *In*: Oceania 37: 148-152.

Malinowski, Bronislaw

1922   Argonauts of the Western Pacific. New York, Dutton; London, Routledge & Kegan Paul. References to 5th impression, 1960.

1926   Crime and Custom in Savage Society. London, Kegan Paul, Trench, Trubner; New York, Harcourt, Brace.

Martin, M. Kay

1969   South American Foragers; a case study in cultural devolution. *In*: American Anthropologist 71: 243-260.

Mauss, Marcel

1924   Essai sur le Don. Forme et Raison de l'Échange dans les Sociétés archaïques. *In*: Année Sociologique, nouv. série I: 30-186. References to Reprint *in* Mauss, 1950.

1950   Sociologie et Anthropologie par Marcel Mauss. Paris, Presses Universitaires de France.

Mead, Margaret

1949   Male and Female. London, Victor Gollancz.

Meggitt, M. J.

1957   Notes on the vegetable Foods of the Walbiri of Central Australia. *In*: Oceania 28: 143-145.

1962   Desert People. A Study of the Walbiri Aborigines. Sydney, Angus & Robertson. References to 1965 reprint, University of Chicago Press.

Meilink-Roelofsz, M. A. P.

1962   Asian Trade and European Influence in the Indonesian Archipelago between 1500 and about 1630. The Hague, Nijhoff.

Onvlee, L.

1973   Cultuur als Antwoord. Verhandelingen van het Ko-